The Dog Lovers' Guides

French Bulldog

Beagle
Boxer
Bulldog
Cavalier King Charles Spaniel
Chihuahua
Cocker Spaniel
Dachshund
French Bulldog
German Shepherd
Golden Retriever
Labrador Retriever
Miniature Schnauzer
Poodle
Pug
Rottweiler
Siberian Husky
Shih Tzu
Yorkshire Terrier

The Dog Lovers' Guides

French Bulldog

By Jennifer Watson

MC

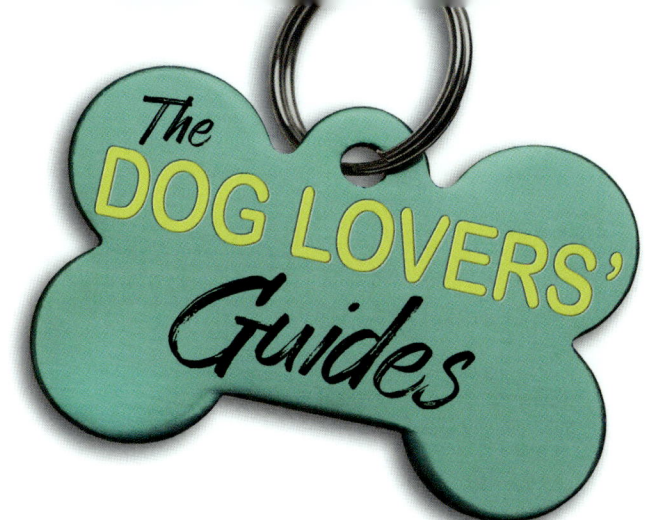

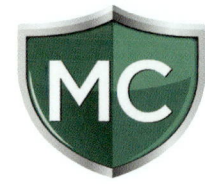

Mason Crest
450 Parkway Drive, Suite D
Broomall, PA 19008
www.masoncrest.com

© 2018 by Mason Crest, an imprint of National Highlights, Inc.

All rights reserved. No part of this publication may be reproduced or transmitted in any form or by any means, electronic or mechanical, including photocopying, recording, taping, or any information storage and retrieval system, without permission from the publisher.

Printed and bound in the United States of America.

Series ISBN: 978-1-4222-3848-6
Hardback ISBN: 978-1-4222-3945-2
EBook ISBN: 978-1-4222-7841-3

First printing
1 3 5 7 9 8 6 4 2

Produced by Shoreline Publishing Group LLC

Cover photograph by Patryk Kosmider/Dreamstime.com.

Library of Congress Cataloging-in-Publication Data is on file with the publisher.

QR Codes disclaimer:

You may gain access to certain third-party content ("Third-Party Sites") by scanning and using the QR Codes that appear in this publication (the "QR Codes"). We do not operate or control in any respect any information, products, or services on such Third-Party Sites linked to by us via the QR Codes included in this publication, and we assume no responsibility for any materials you may access using the QR Codes. Your use of the QR Codes may be subject to terms, limitations, or restrictions set forth in the applicable terms of use or otherwise established by the owners of the Third-Party Sites. Our linking to such Third-Party Sites via the QR Codes does not imply an endorsement or sponsorship of such Third-Party Sites, or the information, products, or services offered on or through the Third-Party Sites, nor does it imply an endorsement or sponsorship of this publication by the owners of such Third-Party Sites.

Contents

1. Introducing the French Bulldog 6
2. What Should a French Bulldog Look Like? 16
3. What Do You Want from Your French Bulldog? ... 26
4. Finding Your Puppy 38
5. A French Bulldog-Friendly Home 48
6. Caring for Your French Bulldog 76
7. Training Your French Bulldog 86
8. Keeping Your Frenchie Busy 104
9. Health Care 110
   Find Out More 126
   Series Glossary of Key Terms 127
   Index 128

Key Icons to Look For

 Sidebars: This boxed material within the main text allows readers to build knowledge, gain insights, explore possibilities, and broaden their perspectives by weaving together additional information to provide realistic and holistic perspectives.

 Educational Videos: Readers can view videos by scanning our QR codes, providing them with additional educational content to supplement the text. Examples include news coverage, moments in history, speeches, iconic moments, and much more!

 Series Glossary of Key Terms: This back-of-the-book glossary contains terminology used throughout this series. Words found here increase the reader's ability to read and comprehend higher-level books and articles in this field.

Chapter 1

Introducing the French Bulldog

Irreverent, affectionate, and a born entertainer, the French Bulldog is the perfect pet for many families. Highly adaptable, he will fit in with lots of different lifestyles, and his unique looks—a Bulldog with bat ears—mean he always stands out in a crowd.

Physical characteristics

Bred down from the larger English Bulldog, the French Bulldog is, in essence, a Bulldog in miniature. He has the typical Bulldog expression, which comes from the short muzzle, the flat, upturned nose, and the undershot jaw. This gives him a pugnacious expression, but it is softened by his round, dark eyes, which convey huge interest in everything that is going on. The French Bulldog's bat ears, which are carried parallel and upright, are a breed specialty, and are very different from the Bulldog, which has rose-shaped ears.

Hugely expressive, the position of the ears will tell you exactly

how your French Bulldog is feeling—which typically ranges from alert, playful, and loving, to on the lookout for mischief! Because the French Bulldog has a very short tail, he cannot signal his feelings that way. But most owners reckon that the French Bulldog has more than made up for this with the unique way he uses his ears.

The French Bulldog has a powerful, muscular body, and is heavy for his size. He should be active and move freely, and will delight you with his sudden, unexpected bursts of energy.

The coat is short, smooth, and easy to care for, and you have a wide choice of colors and combinations.

Brachycephalic breeds

The French Bulldog is brachycephalic breed. Like the Pug, the Pekingese, Boston Terrier, Boxer, and Bulldog, he has a broad, short skull, with a foreshortened muzzle and a pushed-back nose. These features should be distinctive, but never exaggerated. This type of conformation, when exaggerated, can result in serious health problems, including labored breathing.

Some Frenchies are noisy or have labored breathing. They may have a longer tongue or an excessive soft palate that is obstructing their airway. Smaller nose openings can exaggerate their already noisy breathing.

All brachycephalic breeds need extra care in hot weather, when exercise may be trying for them. They also need regular face cleaning and extra care of the skin in and around the facial folds.

The shortened muzzle accounts for another Frenchie specialty—this is a breed that snores! However, most owners find the snuffles and snores of a sleeping dog most endearing.

Temperament

Where to start? French Bulldogs have the most wonderful temperament, and although they share many outstanding characteris-

tics, you will find that every French Bulldog is very much an individual. Breeders use a variety of adjectives to describe the French Bulldog temperament.

- Courageous: The old style English Bulldog was a fighting dog who was set against a tethered bull—a huge animal in comparison—so remarkable courage was a necessity. The Frenchie has inherited his ancestor's fearless approach to life.
- Clown-like: What a brilliant combination to be courageous and yet funny! This is pure French Bulldog—he will take on the world, and make you laugh at the same time.
- Vivacious: This sums up the breed's essential joie de vivre.
- Deeply affectionate: The French Bulldog is a most loving dog who adores his human family. The breed standard describes

the French Bulldog as, "Well behaved, adaptable, and comfortable companions with an affectionate nature and even disposition; generally active, alert, and playful, but not unduly boisterous, being an adaptable and comfortable companion with an even disposition." This underlines how easy it is to live with a French Bulldog.

- Sociable: The French Bulldog gets along well with virtually everyone he comes across, be they human, canine, or feline.
- Playful: Many breeds lose their playfulness as they grow older. Not so the French Bulldog, who will give you endless entertainment as he interacts with all members of his family, and as he goes about his daily life.
- Intelligent: He may not be a star performer in canine sports, but there is no doubting the French Bulldog's mental aptitude. He is a thinking dog who can show great sensitivity.

The ideal home

The Bulldog is a quintessentially British dog, with his pugnacious appearance and steadfast character. Then you add in a French connection, and the result is a unique breed combining power with grace—a dog who is courageous yet loving.

The French Bulldog is a convenient size and has the adaptable nature that means all homes are pretty much the same to him. He will fit into a small apartment and will be equally content in a larger home.

He is well suited to urban life, but he will also enjoy the country. He is a great playmate if you have a young family, but he will also be a loving companion in a quieter household.

In terms of exercise, the French Bulldog is equally adaptable. He will be content with very little, particularly if it is raining. Persuading a French Bulldog to go out when it is wet is quite an undertaking—which shows what sensible dogs they are!

If you are more active, a French Bulldog will enjoy leisurely expeditions, but he is not really built for endurance and should never be over-exercised in warm weather.

Basically, the French Bulldog is a natural when it comes to fitting in. All he asks is to be given lots of love, lots of attention, and to be included in all family activities.

Frenchie history

To trace the history of the French Bulldog you must first go back to his ancestor, the English Bulldog. This dog was lighter in build and had longer legs and muzzle and a smaller head than the Bulldog we know today, as his primary role was as a fighting dog.

For centuries bull baiting was a national pastime in Britain, and crowds of spectators would watch the spectacle of a Bulldog being pitched against a tethered bull. But by the late 1700s, the faster "sport" of dog fighting became even more popular, requiring a more agile dog. Bulldogs were crossed with lightweight, feisty terriers to make the bull-and-terrier breeds used for fighting and ratting. Another group of breeders developed a smaller, lighter toy Bulldog; this dog weighed around 12 to 25 pounds (6 to 11 kg) and had either upright or rose ears (the rose ear folds back at the midway point).

The smaller Bulldogs grew in popularity, and became a favorite among working-class families. The lace makers of Nottingham seemed to have a particular affection for the new breed. When the Industrial Revolution in England closed down many small craft shops, these families migrated to Normandy in France, and they took their dogs with them.

The popularity of these little dogs spread from Normandy to Paris, where they began to be called Bouledogues Français. They were favorites of tradesmen, and in several of his paintings, Toulouse Lautrec included Bouboule, a Frenchie owned by Madame Palmyre, owner of the restaurant La Souris. They also eventually became beloved among the Parisian streetwalkers—and in a very French twist, among the fashionable ladies as well.

As demand grew in the 1880s, trade in these little Bulldogs, which were not so popular in England, increased rapidly, and they became scarce in England while they flourished in France. The French developed a more uniform look to the breed. The Bouledogue Français had a compact body and straight legs, but without the extreme underjaw of the English Bulldog. Some had the erect bat ears, while others had rose ears, which is the ear type seen on English Bulldogs.

Wealthy Americans traveling in France fell in love with these little Bulldogs and began bringing them home. The Americans preferred the bat ears, and the French (and British) preferred the rose ears.

The great ear controversy

A group of American society women and dog fanciers first exhibited Frenchies in 1896 at the Westminster Kennel Club show in New York. Bat-eared and rose-eared dogs were shown together, but the English judge—clearly showing the preferences of his homeland—handed out ribbons only to the rose-eared dogs.

This infuriated the American fanciers, who favored the distinctive look of the bat ear. Very soon after, in 1897, they founded the French Bull Dog Club of America, the very first breed club anywhere in the world to be dedicated to the French Bulldog. They also drew up a breed standard that allowed only the bat ear.

At the 1898 Westminster Kennel Club show, the Americans were outraged to find that both bat-eared and rose-eared dogs were to be

shown—although in separate classes. The new American breed standard allowed only bat ears. It seemed like an insult.

The American judge, and all the American fanciers refused to participate in the show. Instead, the club organized its own show at the luxurious Waldorf-Astoria hotel. Only bat-eared French Bulldogs were allowed. This first specialty show of the French Bull Dog Club of America became famous in the history of the breed, as the moment when ear type was definitively established. (A specialty is a show for just one breed.) The winner of that first specialty was a brindle dog named Dimboolaa.

Frenchies became hugely popular, particularly among society women on the East Coast. And the Americans had the last laugh, because today Frenchies are shown worldwide with bat ears only.

However, like many breeds, numbers dwindled in Europe during World War I, and in America during the Great Depression. In addition, Frenchies have a hard time giving birth naturally, because of the puppies' huge heads, and safe veterinary cesarean sections were not yet routinely performed. By 1940 French Bulldogs were considered a rare breed, and only 100 were registered with the AKC.

New colors

The Frenchies being shown were mostly brindle (a brownish or tawny color, with streaks of other colors), with a few white or

pied (splashes of color on a white background) dogs. Creams and fawns were rare and not particularly popular. That all changed in the 1950s, when a breeder from Detroit, Amanda West, began showing cream Frenchies with phenomenal success. During her show career, her dogs won 111 Bests in Show, and 21 consecutive breed wins at Westminster. From then on, creams and fawns became more and more popular.

French Bulldog history

A breed revived

Only 106 French Bulldogs were registered by the AKC in 1960, and the AKC's magazine lamented that the breed might actually disappear. But in the 1980s, a new generation of breeders re-energized the French Bull Dog Club of America, and by 1990 632 Frenchies were registered in the United States. By 2014, Frenchies cracked the top ten of the AKC's most popular breeds, and came in at number six in 2015 and 2016.

He is once again the favorite of high society, too. Hilary Duff, Lady Gaga, Hugh Jackman, Ashley Olsen, Leonardo DiCaprio, Reese Witherspoon, David and Victoria Beckham, and Martha Stewart all have or had French Bulldogs. The late actress Carrie Fisher was famous for doing television interviews and public appearances with her Frenchie, Gary Fisher, at her side. In an interview she did on *Good Morning America*, Gary became the first guest to fall asleep during the show. The host during that segment, Amy Robach, later said Gary's appearance was "one of the most entertaining interviews of all time."

Chapter 2

What Should a French Bulldog Look Like?

The French Bulldog, with her compact, muscular body, short face, snub nose, and spectacular bat ears, is a striking animal. What should the perfect French Bulldog look like?

The aim of breeders is to produce dogs who are sound, healthy, typical examples of their chosen breed, considering looks, structure, and temperament. To achieve this, they are guided by a breed standard, which is a written blueprint describing the perfect example of the breed. Of course, there is no such thing as a "perfect" dog, but breeders aspire to produce dogs who conform as closely as possible to the picture in words presented by the breed standard. In the show ring, judges use the breed standard to assess the dogs who come before them, and it is the dog who, in their opinion, comes closest to the standard, that wins top honors.

This has significance beyond the sport of showing, because the dogs who win in the ring will be used for breeding. The winners of today are therefore responsible for passing on their genes to future generations and preserving the breed in its best form.

General appearance

This is a small, muscular dog, powerful for her size with heavy, sturdy bones—yet still an active dog. No point should be exaggerated and overall balance should be considered essential. Males and females definitely have a different look (females are less "bully"), although for all Frenchies the breed standard says, "Expression is alert, curious, and interested."

Size

All Frenchies must not exceed 28 pounds (12.7 kg). The distance from the ground to the withers (the top of the shoulder) should be in proportion to the distance from the withers to the root of the tail, "so that animal appears compact, well balanced, and in good proportion," according to the standard.

Temperament

The French Bulldog is a joy to live with. She is sociable and adaptable, and shows deep affection for her family. She is also intelligent, can be courageous, and she loves to play the clown! The breed standard says, "Well behaved, adaptable, and comfortable companions with an affectionate nature and even disposition; generally active, alert, and playful, but not unduly boisterous."

Head and skull

The French Bulldog is known as a "head breed," meaning the magnificent head is a distinguishing feature. It should be large, to be in balance with the powerful neck and sturdy body. The first impression is of squareness—if you measure from the top of the skull to the chin, and then from the outer points of the cheekbones, the distance should be pretty much the same.

The skull should be flat between the ears, with a slightly rounded forehead. The skin should allow for fine wrinkling when the dog is alert. The muzzle is broad. The stop (between the muzzle and the forehead) is "well defined, causing a hollow groove between the eyes with heavy wrinkles forming a soft roll over the extremely short nose." The nostrils should be open and well developed to allow for normal breathing. Nose and lips should be black.

Eyes

The dark eyes should be set relatively wide apart and low on the skull. They are round, and although they may appear prominent, this is discouraged. When a dog is looking forward, no white of eye should be visible.

Ears

The French Bulldog's distinctive bat ears are broad at the base and rounded at the top. They are set high on the head, but should not be too close together. The Frenchie carries her ears erect, and the skin of the ears should be fine and soft to the touch.

Mouth

The lower jaw is deep and square and is slightly undershot, which means that when the mouth is closed the lower teeth rest in front of the upper teeth. The flews are thick and broad, and hang over the lower jaw at the sides.

Neck

The neck is an important feature in achieving the correct balance in conformation. It must be sufficiently strong and thick to join the large head to a short, compact body. There is a small amount of loose skin (dewlap) at the lower jawline, but the underline of the neck should give a clean outline.

Colors and Patterns

The most common colors and patterns are brindle, pied, and fawn.

Fawn: Shades can range from cream to red.

Brindle: A pattern of stripes overlying the fawn shades. A white chest is perfectly acceptable, but more white markings, such as on the face, legs, and back of the neck, are not considered desirable.

Pied: White with splashes of color. The white should always predominate; brindle patches do not need to be symmetrical. In the USA and countries governed by the Federation Internationale Cynologique (FCI), fawn pieds are also allowed, although in the U.K. they are not.

Body

The French Bulldog has a slightly roached back. This means there should be a very slight downward slope between the shoulders; the spine then rises to form a gentle, gradual curve to the root of the tail. The body itself should be short and well-rounded. It should be broader at the shoulders and narrow slightly beyond the ribs, with a tucked-up area at the belly. The overall impression should be compact and powerful.

Forequarters

The front legs are short, muscular, and straight. It is very important that they are set wide apart to give a powerful front, with the chest coming well down between the two legs. The shoulders are short, thick, and muscled; the elbows are held close to the body.

Hindquarters

The hind legs are strong and muscular. They are slightly longer than the front legs, which has the effect of slightly elevating the hindquarters. The hock joint (the ankle) should not be set at too sharp an angle.

Feet are moderate in size, tight and firm. The toes are compact, with high knuckles and short stubby nails. The back feet are a little longer than the front feet.

Tail

The French Bulldog has a naturally short tail, which is set low on the rump. It is thick at the root and tapers to the tip. Ideally, it should be long enough to cover the anus. It can be either straight or screwed, but should not be curly.

Coat

The French Bulldog has a short, shiny, smooth coat with a fine texture. The skin is soft and loose, especially at the head and shoulders, and forms wrinkles.

Colors

The standard allows for many colors and combinations. It says, "All brindle, fawn, white, brindle and white, and any color except those which constitute disqualification. All colors are acceptable with the exception of solid black, mouse, liver, black and tan, black and white, and white with black, which are disqualifications. Black means black without a trace of brindle." All coat colors should be lustrous and clear.

Movement

Despite his muscular build, the French Bulldog's movement should be free and flowing. Viewed from the side, he should use his front and hind legs with equal reach. Movement reveals structure, and absolute soundness should be considered essential.

Summing up

Most French Bulldogs are beloved pets and will never be exhibited in the show ring, but breeders should still strive for perfection and attempt to produce dogs who meet the breed standard. This is the best way of ensuring that the French Bulldog remains sound in mind and body, and retains the characteristics that are unique to this very special breed.

Chapter 3

What Do You Want from Your French Bulldog?

There are hundreds of dog breeds to choose from, so how can you be sure the French Bulldog is the right one for you? Before you run out and get a Frenchie, weigh the pros and cons and make sure you are 100 percent certain this breed suits your lifestyle.

Companion

The French Bulldog is an ideal companion dog; loving and affectionate, he wants nothing more than to be with his people. He is easygoing, tolerant, and adaptable.

If you have a family with small children, the French Bulldog will fit in perfectly. He is not too big and boisterous, but neither is he too small and delicate. He needs to be taught to be calm and sensible

around children, but he seems to have a natural affinity with them and will enjoy joining in their games. In terms of providing entertainment, he is second to none!

The French Bulldog is also a good choice for seniors. He thrives on being the center of attention and will delight in the most low-key events; he is simply happy to be included in everything that is going on. His exercise needs are moderate. He enjoys a leisurely stroll, but he is certainly not built for long and demanding hikes.

Sports dog

If you want to get involved in one of the canine sports, a French Bulldog may not be an obvious choice, but don't write him off! This is an intelligent breed, and if you can make training seem like fun, your French Bulldog will do his part.

Show dog

Do you have ambitions to exhibit your French Bulldog in the show ring? This is a highly competitive sport, so you do need the right dog to begin with.

If you plan to show your French Bulldog you need to track down a show-quality puppy, and train him so he will perform in the show ring and accept the detailed hands-on examination of the judge.

You also need to understand that not every puppy with show potential develops into a top-quality dog. The most promising puppy may not turn out as expected, so you must be prepared to love your Frenchie and give him a home for life, even if he doesn't take home the ribbons.

What does your French Bulldog want from you?

A dog cannot speak for himself, so we need to view the world from a canine perspective and figure out what a French Bulldog needs to live a happy, contented, and fulfilling life.

Time and commitment

First of all, a French Bulldog needs a commitment that you will care for him all his life, guiding him through his puppyhood, enjoying his adulthood, and being there for him in his later years. If all dog owners were prepared to make this pledge, there would hardly be any dogs in shelters and rescue groups.

The French Bulldog is a superb companion dog, but this comes at a price. He loves to be with his own special people, and this means he will be thoroughly miserable if he is excluded from family activities, or is expected to spend long periods on his own.

It is important for all dogs to be able to spend some time on their own without becoming anxious, but the maximum a dog should be left alone is four hours. If this does not fit with your lifestyle, you should put off owning a dog until your circumstances change.

Practical matters

The French Bulldog is a fairly low-maintenance dog. In terms of coat care, his needs are very simple. He is not a great foodie, but if you find a diet that suits him, he will do well. He enjoys his exercise, but this is more in terms of exploring new places rather than going on long marches. For the French Bulldog, variety is the spice of life.

Healthy lifestyle

The Frenchie does not require huge amounts of exercise, which is why he is a good match for older owners or those with less mobility. But if he is allowed to become a couch potato and is fed lots of treats between meals, he will become obese and at risk for serious health problems. It is your responsibility to keep your dog fit and healthy throughout his life.

Training

If you choose a small dog, it is sometimes easy to fall into the trap of thinking training is not really relevant. But no dog, even one as charming as a French Bulldog, instinctively knows how to live in the human world and effortlessly fit into your family.

It is your job to show your French Bulldog how you want him to behave by rewarding the behavior that you consider desirable and not rewarding (even accidentally!) the behavior you don't want him to repeat. You need to be 100 percent consistent, so your French Bulldog is left with no doubt about what you expect.

If he pushes the boundaries or misbehaves, interrupt his undesirable behavior by ignoring him or by refocusing his attention. As soon as your French Bulldog makes the right decision and changes his behavior, you can reward him handsomely.

In this way, your French Bulldog learns good manners without the need for force or coercion. He is living with you in peace and harmony because he loves and respects you.

Mental stimulation

This is a must for all dogs, as boredom can lead to a whole range of behavioral problems. The Frenchie is an intelligent dog, and although he has no desire to be drilled in repetitive exercises, he needs to use his brain to solve problems and learn new things.

Mental stimulation can take many forms—going on different walks so your French Bulldog has the opportunity to discover new and exciting smells, playing games in the yard, or teaching him new tricks. It does not matter what you do; you simply need to remember that a bored dog is an unhappy dog.

Other considerations

Now that you have decided a French Bulldog is the dog for you, you can narrow your choice so you know exactly what you are looking for.

Male or female?

The choice of gender comes down to personal preference. Males are slightly bigger than females, but the difference is not significant. Males also are more Bulldog-like in appearance. In fact, the breed standard says, "In comparing specimens of different sex, due allowance is to be made in favor of bitches, which do not bear the characteristics of the breed to the same marked degree as do the dogs."

In terms of temperament, there is little to choose between the two sexes—both are equally loving and affectionate. Some say females are a little more independent minded, but when it comes down to it, French Bulldogs are all very much individuals.

If you get a female, you will need to cope with her seasons, which will start at any time from six to nine months of age and occur approximately every six months thereafter.

During the three-week period of a season, you will need to keep your bitch away from intact males (males who have not been neutered) to eliminate the risk of an unwanted pregnancy. Some owners also report that females may be a little moody and withdrawn during their seasonal cycle.

Many pet owners spay their female, which puts an end to the seasons and also and has many health benefits. The operation is usually done before the first year. The best plan is to seek advice from your vet.

An intact male may not cause many problems, although some do have a stronger tendency to mark, including inside the house. However, training will usually put a stop to this. An intact male will also be on the lookout for bitches in season, and this may lead to difficulties, depending on your circumstances.

Neutering (castrating) a male is a relatively simple operation, and there are associated health benefits. Again, you should seek advice from your veterinarian.

Color

Health and temperament should be at the top of your list of priorities, but you may well have a preference for a particular color. Fawn offers the greatest choice, as it can range from the palest cream to the darkest red. Dogs may or may not have a black facial mask. Coats with a lot of black hairs are considered undesirable in the show ring, although they do not make a bit of difference for a pet dog.

Brindle shades also range from pale to dark, with or without white markings. Excessive white markings are discouraged, as they are more akin to a Boston Terrier's markings.

More than one?

Owning a French Bulldog can be addictive and you may want to expand your French Bulldog population. However, think carefully before you do. French Bulldogs are sociable dogs and get along with each other perfectly amicably, unless they become jealous over who is getting more of the human attention.

This is a scenario that can arise very easily, particularly if one dog is naturally more pushy. It is therefore your responsibility to ensure that you are even-handed when interacting with your French Bulldogs.

Rehoming a Rescued Dog

We are fortunate that the number of French Bulldogs who end up homeless is relatively small. This may be because the breed is not one of the most popular, or because French Bulldogs are generally easy to live with. However, there are always some French Bulldogs who need a new home, through no fault of their own. The reasons are various, ranging from illness or death of the original owner to family breakdown, changing jobs, or even the arrival of a new baby.

You are unlikely to find a French Bulldog in an all-breed shelter; contacting a Frenchie breed club that runs a rescue group will be your best option if you want to adopt a homeless Frenchie.

Try to find out as much as you can about a dog's history, so you know exactly what you are taking on. You need to be aware of age and health status, likes and dislikes, and any behavioral issues. You need to be realistic about what you are capable of achieving, so you can be sure you can give the dog in question a permanent home.

Regardless of the dog's previous history, you will need to give him plenty of time and be patient with him as he settles into his new home. It may take weeks, or even months before he becomes fully integrated in the family. But if all goes well, you will have the reward of knowing that you have given a French Bulldog a second chance.

The best plan is to go for a male and a female, as they are most likely to form a bond and will have less of a need to challenge each other. One, or preferably both, dogs will need to be neutered, or you'll have puppies at every season.

Take care with initial introductions, and make sure you are very aware of the way the two dogs react to each other, particularly when they are vying for attention from their human family.

Be wary of a breeder who encourages you to buy two puppies from the same litter, as it is unlikely that the welfare of the puppies is their top priority. Most responsible breeders have a waiting list of potential purchasers before a litter is even born and have no need to make this type of sale.

If you do decide to get a second French Bulldog, wait at least 18 months, until your first dog is fully trained and grown up, before looking for another puppy.

An adult dog

You may decide to skip the puppy phase and get an adult dog instead. Such a dog may be harder to track down, but sometimes a breeder may have a youngster who is not suitable for showing, but is perfect for a family pet. The breeder may have kept a promising puppy, but the pup just didn't turn out as expected. Such dogs are typically well trained and well socialized by the time the breeder decides to let them go, and make great companions.

In some cases, a breeder may rehome a female when her breeding career is at an end, so she will enjoy the benefits of more individual attention. Or they may decide to let a retired show dog be pampered in a pet home.

There are advantages to taking on an adult dog, as you know exactly what you are getting. But the upheaval of changing homes can be quite upsetting, so you will need to have plenty of patience during the settling-in period.

Chapter 4

Finding Your Puppy

Your aim is to find a healthy French Bulldog puppy who has been bred and reared with the greatest possible care. Where do you begin?

One way is to attend a dog show where French Bulldogs are being exhibited. The classes are divided between males and females and by ages, so you will see puppies from as young as six months, veterans, and everything in between. You will be able to see a wide range of colors and markings and, if you look closely, you will also see there are differences in type. They are all purebred French Bulldogs, but breeders produce dogs with a family likeness, so you can see which type you prefer.

When the judging is finished, talk to the exhibitors and find out more about their dogs. They may not have puppies available, but some will be planning a litter, and you may decide to put your name on a waiting list.

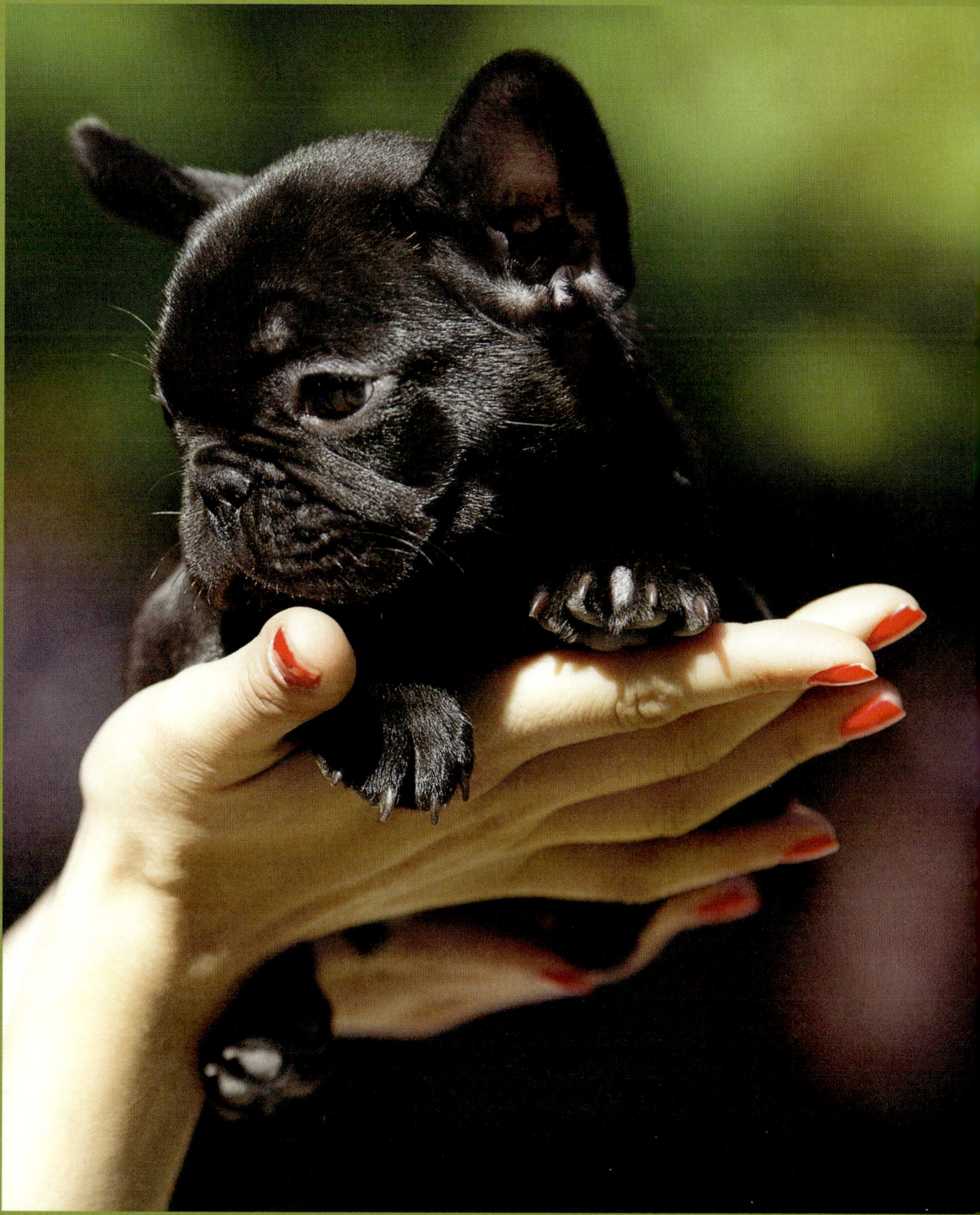

Internet research

The Internet is an excellent resource, but when it comes to finding a puppy, use it with care.

Do go to the websites of both the American Kennel Club (AKC) and the United Kennel Club (UKC), which will give you information about the French Bulldog as a breed, and what to look for when choosing a puppy. You will also find contact details for breed clubs.

Both sites may have lists of breeders, and you can look for breeders of merit from the AKC, which indicates that a code of conduct has been followed.

Do go to the sites of the national and local breed clubs. On breed club websites you will find lots of useful information that will help you to care for your French Bulldog. There may be contact details of breeders in your area. Some websites also have a list of breeders who have puppies available. The advantage of going through a breed club is that members will follow a code of ethics, and this will give you some guarantees regarding the puppy's parents and health checks.

If you are planning to show your French Bulldog, you will need to find a breeder that specializes in show lines and has a reputation for producing top-quality dogs.

Remember that health and temperament are top priorities, so do not overlook these considerations when you are researching pedigrees.

Do not look at puppies for sale. There are legitimate French Bulldog breeders with their own websites, and they may, occasionally advertise a litter, although in most cases reputable breeders have waiting lists for their puppies before they are even born.

The danger comes from unscrupulous breeders who produce puppies purely for profit, with no thought for the health of the dogs they breed and no care given to rearing the litter.

Photos of puppies are hard to resist, but never make a decision based purely on an online advertisement. You need to find out who the breeder is, and have the opportunity to visit their premises and inspect the litter before making a decision.

Responsible breeders

Responsible breeders raise their puppies at home and underfoot. They have one or, at the most, two litters at a time. They carefully study the pedigrees of the male and female before they arrange any breeding, with an eye toward breeding the healthiest, most temperamentally sound dogs. Responsible breeders belong to a breed club and are involved in their breed.

Responsible breeders register their puppies with a well-established registry such as the AKC or the UKC. (Registration with a well-established kennel club is a guarantee that your French Bulldog is truly a French Bulldog, but it is not a guarantee of good health or temperament.) They are able to hand over registration documents at the time of sale. Their breeding dogs are permanently identified by microchip or DNA. They screen them for hereditary health problems, and can tell you exactly which screening tests their dogs have had and what the results were.

You should be able to meet the mother and see where the puppies are kept. Everything should look and smell clean and healthy. The mother should be a well-socialized dog. She may be a little protective of her babies, but she should act like a typical French Bulldog.

Responsible breeders socialize all their puppies in a home environment. They provide written advice on feeding, ongoing training, socialization, parasite control, and vaccinations. They are available for phone calls after you buy their puppies, and will take a dog back at any time. They have a written contract of sale for each puppy that conforms to your state's laws.

Questions, questions, questions

When you find a responsible breeder with puppies available, you will have lots of questions to ask. These should include:

- Where have the puppies been reared? Hopefully, they will be in a home environment, which gives them the best possible start in life.
- How many males and females are in the litter?

- How many have already been spoken for? The breeder will probably be keeping a puppy to show or for breeding, and there may be other people on a waiting list.
- Can I see the mother with her puppies?
- What age are the puppies now?
- When will they be ready to go to their new homes?

Bear in mind that puppies need to be with their mother and siblings until they are a minimum of 10 weeks of age. Otherwise they miss out on vital learning and communication skills, which will have a detrimental effect on them for the rest of their lives.

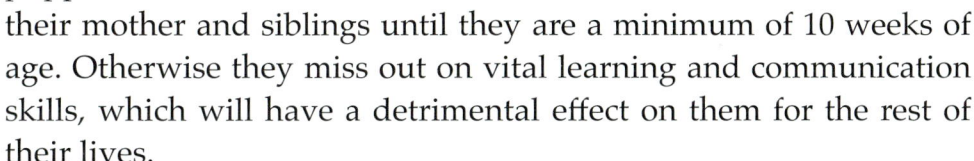

The breeder should also have lots and lots of questions for you. Don't be offended! They take seriously their responsibility for every puppy they produce, and that's a good thing.

You will be asked some or all of the following questions:
- What is your home setup?
- Do you have children or grandchildren? What are their ages?
- Is there somebody at home most of the time?
- What is your previous experience with dogs?
- Do you already have other dogs at home?
- Do you want to show your French Bulldog?
- Do you have plans to compete with your French Bulldog in one of the canine sports?

The breeder is not being intrusive; they need to understand the type of home you will provide so they can make the right match. The breeder is doing it for both the dog's benefit and also for yours.

Steer clear of a breeder who does not ask you questions. He or she may be more interested in making money from the puppies than ensuring that they go to good homes. They may also have taken other short cuts, which may prove disastrous, and very expensive, in terms of vet bills and heartache.

Health issues

Like all purebred dogs, the French Bulldog suffers from some hereditary problems. Ask the breeder for a full history of the parents and preceding generations to see if there are any problems you need to be aware of. Ask to see health clearances as well.

The French Bull Dog Club of America recommends for all breeding animals: evaluation for hip dysplasia, patellar luxation, and autoimmune thyroiditis; a congenital cardiac exam;

a DNA test for juvenile cataracts; an annual eye exam with a board-certified ophthalmologist.

Puppy watching

French Bulldog puppies are totally irresistible. Looking like adults in miniature, they are brimming with personality, and each puppy seems to be saying: "Take me home!" However, you must try to put your feelings aside so that you can make an informed choice.

Always remember that you are making a long-term commitment. You need to be 100 percent confident that the parents are healthy, and the puppies have been reared with love and care, before making a commitment to buy.

It is a good idea to have a mental checklist of what to look for when you visit a breeder. You want to see:
- A clean, hygienic environment.
- Puppies who are outgoing, friendly, and eager to meet you.
- A sweet-natured mother who is ready to show off her puppies.
- Pups who are well fleshed-out but not pot-bellied (which could be an indication of worms).
- Bright eyes, with no sign of soreness or discharge.
- Clean ears that smell fresh.
- No discharge from the eyes or nose.
- Clean rear ends—matting could indicate upset tummies.
- Lively pups who are keen to play.

It is important that you see the mother with her puppies, as this will give you a good idea of the temperament they are likely to inherit.

In most cases, you will not be able to see the father (sire) as most breeders will travel some distance to find a stud dog who is not too close to their own bloodlines and complements their bitch. However, you should be able to see photos of him and examine his pedigree, which will help you to make an informed decision.

French Bulldogs on show

Companion puppy

If you are looking for a French Bulldog as a companion, you should be guided by the breeder, who will have spent hours and hours puppy watching, and will know each of the pups as an individual. It is tempting to choose a puppy yourself, but the breeder will take into account your family and lifestyle and will help you to pick the most suitable puppy.

Show puppy

If you are buying a puppy with the hope of showing him, make this clear to the breeder. A lot of planning goes into producing a litter, and although all the puppies will have been reared with equal care, there will be one or two who have show potential.

Ideally, recruit a breed expert to meet the puppies with you, to get their objective evaluation. The breeder will also be helpful, since they will want to make sure only their best dogs are exhibited in the show ring. Wait until the puppies are between seven and eight weeks before making your choice, as this gives them time to develop.

By the time the puppies are six weeks old, their ears should be erect. French Bulldog puppies are born with their ears down, and they start to go up from four weeks onward, though they can be up one minute and down the next for a few weeks. Teething, which occurs at around four months, will also affect ear carriage.

The head should be fairly large and wide, with a broad muzzle. The correct jaw is important in the breed; by eight weeks, the teeth on the lower jaw close over the teeth on the upper jaw.

French Bulldogs are born with a short tail, and sometimes no tail at all. This occurs naturally; tails are never docked. Sometimes the tail will stick straight out in a young puppy, but this generally lies flat as the dog matures. A tail that sticks straight up is likely to stay that way, and, although this is fine for a pet, it would not be acceptable in the show ring.

A puppy will go through many stages as he is growing up—the most beautiful puppy can grow through an ugly duckling phase. However, if the basic conformation is correct, there is a good chance your pup will mature into a sound, typical representative of the breed.

Chapter 5

A French Bulldog-Ready Home

It may seem like forever before your puppy is ready to leave the breeder and come home with you. But you can fill the time by getting your home ready and buying the equipment you will need. These preparations apply to a new puppy but, in reality, they are the way you will create an environment that is safe and secure for your French Bulldog throughout his life.

At home

Nothing is safe when a puppy is about—and this is certainly true of the inquisitive French Bulldog. Everything is new and exciting for a young puppy. It all needs thorough investigation—and this usually means testing with mouth and teeth. One thing is certain—an

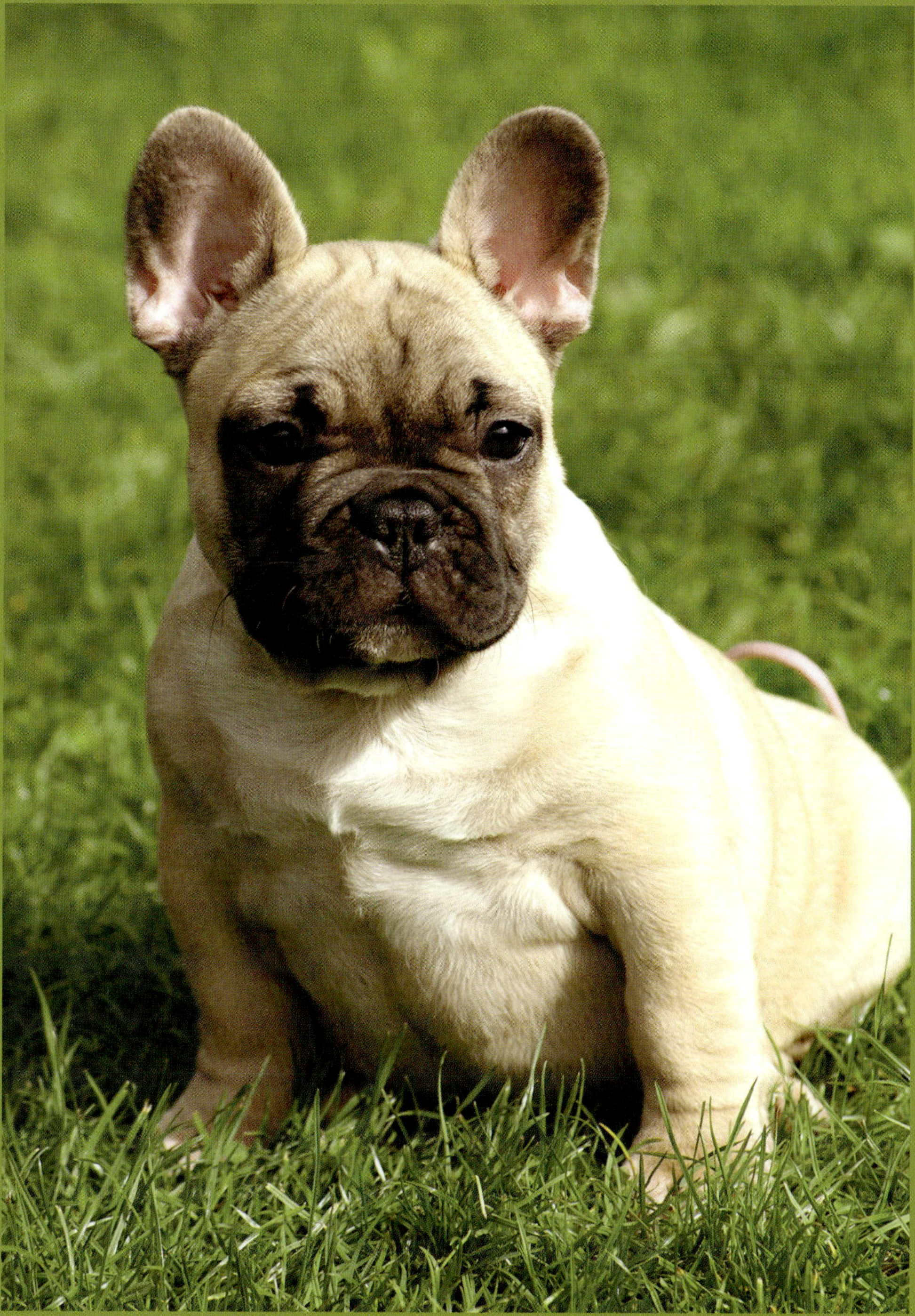

unsupervised French Bulldog puppy cannot be trusted! Remember, it is not only your prized possessions that are under threat; so is your puppy, who can accidentally hurt himself quite seriously.

    Look around and ask yourself what mischief a puppy could get up to and what he could chew. Electric cords are prime candidates, so these should be safely secured where a puppy cannot reach them. Try running exposed cords and cables through PVC pipe to keep little teeth away. Anything breakable, such as glass or china, is very dangerous—once broken by a wagging tail, a puppy could step on sharp pieces or even swallow them. Houseplants also need to be out of reach, as, even if they are not poisonous, they will very likely upset a puppy's tummy.

    You will need to make sure all cupboards and storage units cannot be opened—or broken into. This applies particularly in the kitchen and bathroom, where you may store cleaning materials and other substances that are toxic to dogs.

If you have stairs, it would be wise to declare upstairs off-limits. Negotiating stairs can be hazardous and puts unnecessary stress on a puppy's growing joints. The best way to do this is to put a baby gate at the bottom of the stairs—but make sure your puppy can't squeeze through it or under it when he is very small.

In the yard

A French Bulldog does not have a great desire to roam, but curiosity can get the better of him, and he may find his way out of insubstantial fencing. If you plan to let your dog out in the yard without a leash, make sure it's safe for the new arrival. Check that there are no holes in the fence or gaps underneath that a puppy can escape through, and also check that gates leading out of your property have secure fastenings.

Be aware of chemicals you may have in your yard, such as fertilizer for the lawn, or weed or bug killer. Any of these, if eaten by a dog, could be fatal. Keep all toxic substances in a secure place, well out of reach. Rat poison, slug pellets, and antifreeze are particularly dangerous. Find out if your garden contains plants that are poisonous to dogs. There is not enough room to list them all here, but you can find a full list at www.aspca.org/pet-care/animal-poison-control/toxic-and-non-toxic-plants.

Swimming pools and ponds should be covered, as most puppies are fearless and, although it is easy for a puppy to take the plunge, it is virtually impossible for him to get out—which could prove fatal. You will also need to designate a toileting area. This will assist the housetraining process, and it will also make cleaning up easier.

House rules

Before your puppy comes home, hold a family conference to decide on the house rules. You need to decide which rooms your puppy will have access to, and establish whether he is allowed on the furniture or not. The most important thing is to be consistent, so your French Bulldog understands the rules. He will be very confused if one member of the family allows him on the sofa for a cuddle and then someone else tells him to get off—or if you let him up for a cuddle when he's a puppy but change your mind when he is an adult.

Start as you mean to go on. The French Bulldog likes to please, but he will push it if he doesn't know where his boundaries are. If house rules are applied consistently, he will understand what is and what is not allowed.

Going shopping

There are some essential items you will need for your Frenchie. If you choose wisely, much of it will last for many years to come.

Indoor crate

Rearing a puppy is so much easier if you invest in an indoor crate. It provides a safe haven for your puppy at night, when you have to go out during the day, and at other times when you cannot supervise him. A puppy needs a base where he feels safe and secure, and where he can rest undisturbed. An indoor crate provides the perfect den, and many adult dogs continue to use them throughout their lives. You need to buy a crate that will be big enough to accommodate your French Bulldog when he is fully grown. He must be able to stand up and turn around.

You will also need to think about where you are going to put the crate. The kitchen is often the most suitable place, as this is the hub of family life. Find a snug corner where the puppy can rest when he wants to, but where he can also see what is going on around him and still be with the family.

Beds and bedding

The crate will need to be lined with bedding, and the best type to buy is synthetic fleece. This is warm and cozy, and because moisture soaks through it, your puppy will not have a wet bed when he is tiny and is still unable to go through the night without relieving himself. This type of bedding is machine washable and easy to dry; buy two pieces, so you have one to use while the other piece is in the wash.

If you have purchased a crate, you may not feel the need to buy an extra bed, although your French Bulldog may like to have a bed in the family room so he feels part of household activities. There is an amazing array of dog beds to chose from—sofas, bean bags, cushions, baskets, igloos, mini-four posters—so you can take your pick! Bear in mind that some beds prove irresistible as far as chewing is concerned, so put off making a major investment until your French Bulldog has outgrown the teething phase.

Collar and leash

You may think that it is not worth buying a collar for the first few weeks, but the sooner your pup gets used to it, the better. A nylon lightweight collar is fine, as most puppies will accept it without making a fuss. Be careful when you are fitting the collar that is not too tight, but equally not too loose, as slipping the collar can become a favorite game. A good guideline is to make sure you can fit two fingers under the collar.

A thin, matching woven nylon leash will be fine to begin with. You don't want your puppy to feel weighed down by a heavy collar and leash.

An extending leash can be useful to give your French Bulldog limited freedom when it is not safe or permitted to allow him off-leash. However, you should never use it when walking on the street. If your French Bulldog pulls unexpectedly and the leash extends more than you intend, it could have disastrous consequences.

ID

Your French Bulldog needs to wear some form of ID when he is out in public. This can be a tag engraved with your contact details and attached to the collar. When your French Bulldog is full-grown, you can buy an embroidered collar with your contact details, which eliminates the danger of the tag falling off.

You may also wish to consider a permanent form of ID. Increasingly, breeders are getting puppies microchipped before they go to their new homes. A microchip is the size of a grain of rice. It is injected under the skin, usually between the shoulder blades, with a special needle.

Each chip has its own unique identification number that can only be read by a special scanner. That ID number is then registered on a national database with your name and details, so if your dog is lost, any veterinarian or shelter where he is scanned can contact you. If your puppy has not been microchipped, you can ask your vet to do it, maybe when he goes in for his vaccinations.

Bowls

Your French Bulldog will need two bowls; one for food, and one for fresh drinking water, which should always be readily available. A stainless steel bowl is a good choice for a food bowl. Plastic bowls will almost certainly be chewed, and there is a danger that bacteria can collect in the small cracks that may appear. You can get a second stainless steel bowl for drinking water, or you may prefer a heavier ceramic bowl, which will not be knocked over so easily.

Food

The breeder will let you know what your puppy is eating and should provide a full diet sheet to guide you through the first six months of your puppy's feeding regime—how much he is eating per meal, how many meals per day, when to increase the amounts per meal, and when to reduce the meals per day.

The breeder may provide you with some food when you pick up your puppy, but it is worth making inquiries in advance about the availability of the brand that is recommended.

Toys

French Bulldog puppies love to play, and there is no shortage of dog toys on the market. But before you get carried away buying a vast range of toys to keep your puppy entertained, you need to think about which are the safest. Plastic toys can be shredded, cuddly toys can be chewed, and toys where the squeaker can be removed should be avoided at all costs. If your French Bulldog ingests part of a toy, it could well result in an internal blockage, and the results of this are often fatal.

The safest toys to choose are made of hard rubber; a rubber Kong that can be stuffed with food is ideal. You can also buy rope tug toys, but be careful how you play with your dog, particularly while he is teething. French Bulldogs also like to play with balls. Again, go for a rubber ball and make sure it is big enough that it cannot be swallowed.

Grooming gear

The French Bulldog is a fairly low-maintenance breed in terms of coat, but there are a few bare essentials you will need:
- Soft brush to use while your puppy is getting accustomed to grooming
- Hound glove/rubber brush for adult coat care
- Nail-clippers—the guillotine type are easy to use
- Toothbrush and toothpaste—choose between a long-handled toothbrush or a finger brush, whichever you find easiest to use; there are flavored canine toothpastes your dog will love
- Cotton balls and pads for cleaning the eyes, ears, and facial wrinkles
- Petroleum jelly to apply after cleaning the wrinkles

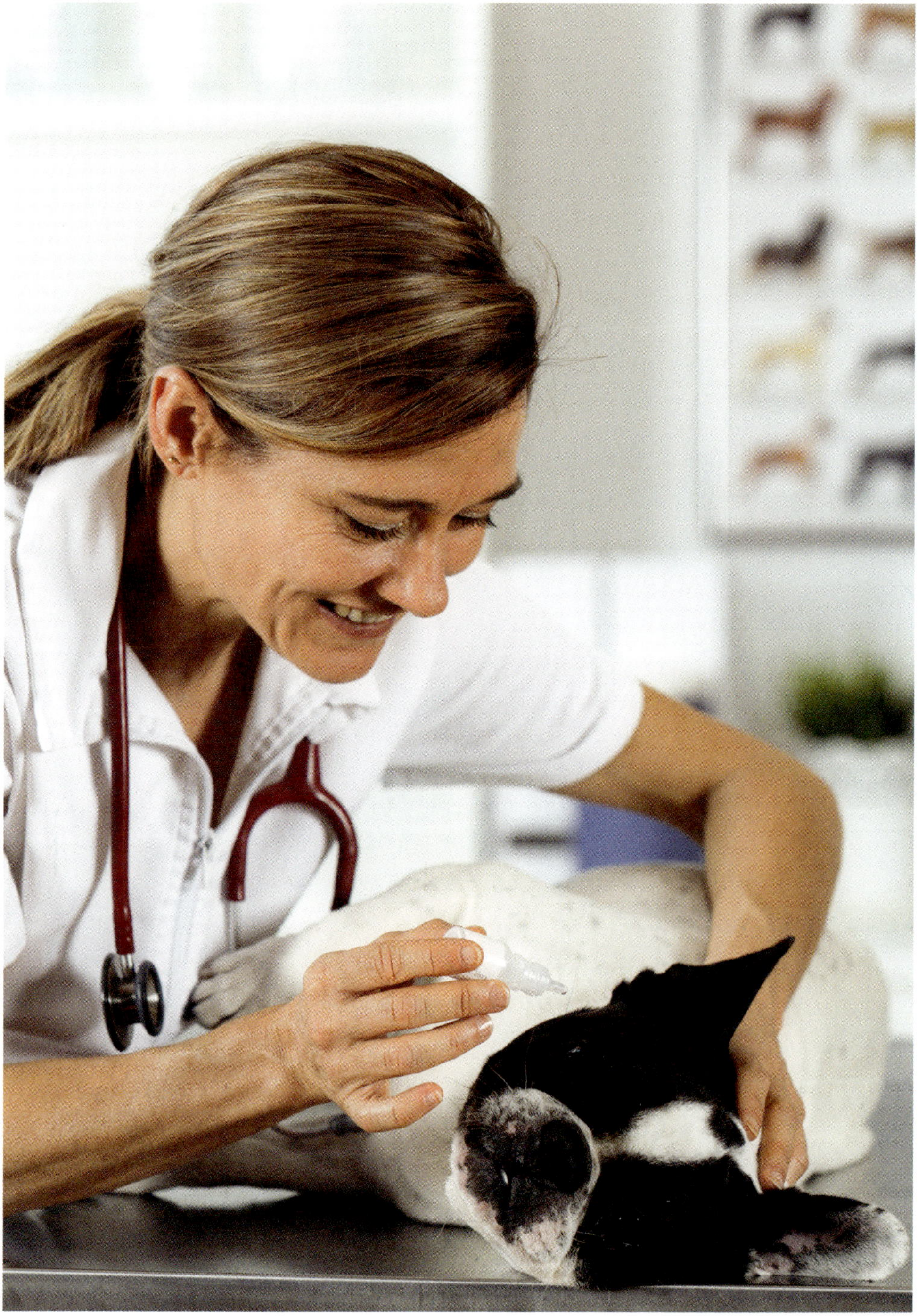

Finding a veterinarian

Do this before you bring your dog home, so you have a vet to call if there is a problem. Visit some of the vets in your area, and speak to other pet owners to find out who they recommend. It is as important to find a good vet as it is to find a good doctor for yourself. You need to find someone with whom you can build a good rapport and have complete faith in. Word of mouth is really the best recommendation.

When you contact a veterinary practice, find out:
- What facilities are available at the practice?
- What are the details of emergency and after-hours care?
- Do the vets in the practice have experience treating Frenchies?

If you are satisfied with what you find, and the staff appear to be helpful and friendly, book an appointment so your puppy can have a health check a couple of days after you bring him home. The vet will need to see the vaccination record and will record all the details both for you and the dog. He or she will discuss with you feeding, worming, parasite treatments, and probably microchipping, at the first visit.

Settling in

When you first arrive home with your puppy, be careful not to overwhelm him. You and your family are hugely excited, but the puppy is in a completely unfamiliar environment with new sounds, smells, and sights. This is a daunting experience, even for the boldest of pups.

Some puppies are very confident, wanting to play right away and quickly making friends; others need a little longer. Keep a close eye on your French Bulldog's body language and reactions so you can proceed at a pace he is comfortable with.

When you take your puppy indoors, let him investigate. Show him his crate, and encourage him to enter by throwing in a treat. Let him sniff, and allow him to go in and out as he wants. Later on, when he is tired, you can put him in the crate while you stay in the room. This way, he will learn to settle and will not think he is being abandoned.

It is a good idea to feed your puppy in his crate, at least to begin with, as this helps to build up a positive association. It will not be long before your French Bulldog sees his crate as his own special den and will go there on his own. Some owners place a blanket over the crate, covering the back and sides, so that it is even more cozy and den-like.

Meeting the family

Resist the temptation to invite friends and neighbors to come and meet the new arrival. Your puppy needs to focus on getting to know his new family for the first few days. Try not to swamp your French Bulldog with too much attention—he needs a chance to explore and find his own way. There will be plenty of time for cuddles later on!

If you have children in the family, you need to keep everything as calm as possible. Your puppy may not have met children before, and even if he has, he will still find them strange and unpredictable. A puppy can become alarmed by too much noise, or he may go to the opposite extreme and become over-excited, which can lead to mouthing and nipping.

The best plan is to get the children to sit on the floor and give them all a treat. Each child can then call the puppy, stroke him, and offer a treat. This way, the puppy is making the decisions rather than being forced into interactions he may find stressful.

If he tries to nip or mouth, make sure there is a toy ready nearby, so his attention can be diverted to something he is allowed to bite. If you do this consistently, he will learn to inhibit his desire to mouth when he is interacting with people.

Right from the start, impose a rule that the children are not allowed to pick up or carry the puppy. They can cuddle him when they are sitting on the floor. This may sound a little severe, but a wriggly puppy can be dropped in an instant, sometimes with disastrous consequences.

If possible, try to make sure your French Bulldog only gets attention when he has all four feet on the ground. This is a breed than can be attention-seeking, so if your pup learns that jumping up and demanding attention is not rewarding, it will pay dividends later on.

Involve all family members with your puppy's day-to-day care. This will develop his bond with the whole family, as opposed to just one person. Encourage the children to train and reward the puppy, so he learns to follow cues from everyone in the family.

The animal family

Great care must be taken when introducing a puppy to a resident dog, to ensure that relations get off on the right footing. French Bulldogs do have a jealous streak, so you need to be even-handed in all your interactions. If the two dogs are confident of their place in your affections, they will not need to vie for your attention.

Ideally, introduce your resident dog to the newcomer at the breeder's home. This works well because the puppy feels secure and the adult dog does not feel threatened. But if this is not possible, allow your dog to smell the puppy's bedding (bedding supplied by the breeder is fine) before they actually meet, so he familiarizes himself with the puppy's scent.

Outdoors is the best place to introduce the puppy, since the adult will regard it as neutral territory. He will probably take a great interest in the puppy and sniff him all over. Most puppies are naturally submissive in this situation, and your pup may lick the other dog's mouth or roll over on to his back. Try not to interfere, as this is the natural way dogs get to know each other.

You will only need to intervene if the older dog is too boisterous, and alarms the puppy. In this case, it is a good idea to put the adult on his leash so you have some measure of control.

It rarely takes long for an adult to accept a puppy, since he does not constitute a threat. This will be underlined if you make a big fuss over the older dog, so he has no reason to feel jealous. But no matter how well the two dogs are getting along, do not leave them alone unless one is crated.

Feline friends

The French Bulldog is a tolerant animal and he will learn to live peaceably with the family cat. There will always be moments when he can't resist a chase, but most of the time cat and dog will coexist peacefully.

However, it is important to supervise early interactions so everyone remains safe. Bear in mind that a French Bulldog has large, fairly prominent eyes, and one swipe from a cat's claw could cause a lot of damage. Keep the dog on a leash for the first couple of meetings so your puppy has a chance to make his acquaintance in a controlled situation. Keep calling your puppy to you and rewarding him so that he does not get obsessed with cat watching. When you allow your puppy to go free, make sure the cat has an easy escape route, just in case the dog tries to chase.

This is an ongoing process, but all the time your French Bulldog is learning that he is rewarded for ignoring the cat. In time, the novelty will wear off and the pair will live in peace—who knows, they may even become friends!

The most important thing you can do is make sure your cat has plenty of elevated spots in every room, well out of the puppy's reach, to which she can retreat. Feed her up high, as well, so she will not be bothered. And if the puppy is showing too much interest in her litter box, put it in a room that is blocked with a baby gate, so kitty can go over but the puppy can't get in.

Feeding

The breeder will generally provide enough food for the first few days, so your puppy does not have to cope with a change in diet—and possible digestive upset—along with all the stress of moving to a new home.

Some puppies eat up their food from the very first meal; others are more concerned about their new surroundings and are too distracted to eat. Do not worry if your puppy seems uninterested in his food for the first day or so. Give him 10 minutes to eat what he wants and then remove the leftovers and give him fresh food at the next meal. Obviously, if you have any concerns about your puppy in the first few days, seek advice from your veterinarian.

French Bulldogs can sometimes become possessive, and this behavior can be seen at mealtimes if a Frenchie is insecure and feels the need to guard his food bowl. It is therefore important that you give your dog a space where he can eat in peace, and if you have children, you must establish a rule that no one is to go near the dog when he is eating. This is common sense, and removes all risk of problems arising, no matter how unintentional they may be.

You can also work on your French Bulldog's manners so that he does not feel protective of his food bowl. You can do this by giving him half his meal, and then dropping food around his bowl. This will prevent him from guarding his bowl and, at the same time, he will see your presence in a positive light.

You can also call him away from the bowl and reward him with some food—maybe something extra special—which he can take from your hand. Start doing this as soon as your puppy arrives in his new home, and continue working on it throughout his life.

The first night

Your puppy will have spent his entire life so far with his mother or curled up with his siblings. He is then taken from everything he knows as familiar, lavished with attention by his new family—and then comes bedtime when he is left all alone. It is little wonder that he feels abandoned!

The best plan is to establish a nighttime routine, and then stick to it so that your puppy knows what is expected of him. Take your puppy outside to relieve himself, and then settle him in his crate. Some people leave a low light on for the puppy at night for the first week, others have tried soft music as company or a ticking clock. A covered hot-water bottle filled with warm water can also be a comfort. Like people, puppies are all individuals and what works for one, does not necessarily work for another, so it is a matter of trial and error.

Be very positive when you leave your puppy on his own. Do not linger or keep returning; this will make the situation more difficult. It is inevitable that he will protest to begin with, but if you stick to your routine, he will accept that he gets left at night—but you always return in the morning.

Rescued dogs

Settling an adult rescued dog in the home is very similar to a puppy, in as much as you will need to make the same preparations for his homecoming. As with a puppy, an adult dog will need you to be consistent, so start as you mean to go on.

There is often an initial honeymoon period when you bring a rescued dog home, where he will be on his best behavior for the first few weeks. It is after these first couple of weeks that the true nature of the dog will show, so be prepared for subtle changes.

It may be advisable to register with a reputable dog trainer or a training club, so you can seek advice on any training or behavioral issues at an early stage.

Above all, remember that a rescued dog ceases to be a rescued dog the moment he enters his forever home with you.

Housetraining

This is an aspect of training that first-time owners dread, but if you start as you mean to go on, it will not be long before your French Bulldog understands what is required. The key to successful housetraining is vigilance and consistency. If you establish a routine and you stick to it, your puppy will understand what is required.

Equally, you must be there to supervise him at all times—except when he is safely tucked away in his crate. It is when a puppy is left to wander from room to room that accidents are most likely to happen.

You will have allocated a toileting area in your yard or somewhere else outdoors when preparing for your puppy's homecoming. Take your puppy to this area every time he needs to relieve himself so he builds up an association and knows why you have brought him outside.

Establish a routine and make sure you take your puppy out at the following times:
- First thing in the morning
- After mealtimes
- When he wakes up
- After a play session
- Last thing at night

Tips on housetraining a puppy.

A puppy should be taken out to relieve himself every two hours as an absolute minimum. If you can manage an hourly trip out, so much the better. The more often your puppy gets it right, the quicker he will learn to be clean in the house. It helps if you use a verbal cue, such as "busy," when your pup is performing, and in time, this will trigger the desired response.

Do not be tempted to put your puppy out on the doorstep to the backyard in the hope that he will toilet on his own. Most pups simply sit there, waiting to get back inside the house! No matter how bad the weather is, accompany your puppy and give him lots of praise when he performs correctly. Do not rush back inside as soon as he has finished; your puppy might start to delay in the hope of prolonging his time outside with you. Praise him, have a quick game—and then you can both return indoors.

When accidents happen

No matter how vigilant you are, there are bound to be accidents. If your puppy has an accident, always ask yourself: Did I give him enough opportunity? What should I do differently?

If you witness the accident, take your puppy outside immediately, and give him lots of praise if he finishes his business out there. If you are not there when he has an accident, do not scold him when you discover what has happened. He will not remember what he has done and will not understand why you are angry with him. Simply clean it up and resolve to be more vigilant next time.

Make sure you use a cleaner that's made for pet urine when you clean up. Otherwise your pup will be drawn to the smell and may be tempted to use the same spot again.

Choosing a diet

A well-balanced diet is key to your dog's health and well-being, so you need to learn a few things about dog food. There are so many different types of food, all claiming to be the best. But which is the best for your French Bulldog?

Dry food

Most dry foods, or kibble, are scientifically formulated to meet all your dog's nutritional needs. Kibble is certainly convenient, and is often less expensive than other diets.

There are many brands of kibble available, and most offer life-stage foods, such as puppy, adult, and senior. There are also special diets for pregnant bitches, working dogs, and prescription diets for weight control, and other health-related conditions.

Which kibble is best? This is a difficult question, and the best plan is to seek advice from your puppy's breeder or your veterinarian. Generally, an adult maintenance diet should contain 21 to 24 percent protein and 10 to 14 percent fat. Protein levels should be higher in puppy diets, and reduced in senior diets.

Most kibble has some kind of grain in it to form the pieces. Bear in mind that wheat products are known to produce flatulence in some French Bulldogs. Corn products and fillers that are an additional source of protein may cause skin rashes or irritations.

Kibble can be fed on its own, or along with other types of food. It is best fed in a puzzle toy—a toy dogs must manipulate in some way to get the food out. No dog is too young—or too old!—to start eating kibble from a puzzle toy.

Canned food and pouches

Canned food contains a lot more water than kibble. Some canned foods—although certainly not all—will have fewer carbohydrates than kibble. The more natural wet foods contain rice rather than other cereals containing gluten, so select this type to avoid allergic reactions. Read the label carefully so you are aware of the ingredients and, remember, what you put in will affect what comes out.

Canned food can be all or part of your dog's diet. Even if it is only a part, the label should say the diet is complete and balanced for your dog.

Homemade

There are some owners who like to prepare meals especially for their dogs—and it is probably much appreciated. The danger is that although the food is tasty, and your French Bulldog may appreciate the variety, you cannot be sure that it has the correct nutritional balance. There are a lot of homemade diet recipes on the Internet, but recent research has found that the majority of them do not offer complete and balanced nutrition.

If this is a route you want to go down, you will need to find out the exact ratio of fats, carbohydrates, proteins, minerals, and vitamins that are needed, which is quite an undertaking.

Commercially prepared raw diets may come fresh or frozen or freeze-dried, or you might choose to prepare your dog's diet yourself. They typically contain raw meat, bones, organ meats, fat, vegetables, and sometimes, some cooked grains. Proponents of raw diets believe they are providing the dog with a food that is very close to the natural diet he would eat in the wild.

If you're buying a commercial raw diet, look for a statement on the label that says it's complete and balanced. If you want to prepare the diet yourself, work with a veterinary nutritionist to formulate a healthy diet for your dog.

Feeding schedule

When your puppy arrives in his new home he will need four meals, evenly spaced throughout the day. You may decide to stick with the food recommended by your puppy's breeder, and if your pup is thriving there is no need to change. However, if your puppy is not doing well on the food, or you have problems with supply, you will need to make a change.

When switching diets, it is very important to do it gradually, changing over from one food to the next a little at a time, and spreading the transition over a week to 10 days. This will avoid the risk of digestive upset.

Your dog's food should be spread over three meals a day, decreasing to two meals of an adult maintenance diet when the dog is fully mature. Breeds vary in the length of time they take to reach full maturity; French Bulldogs should be considered full adults at around two years of age. As discussed, puppies need a higher ratio of protein than adult dogs, and dogs age 9 to 18 months will need more food than a mature adult.

Picky eaters

The French Bulldog is not passionate about his food, and so there is the very real danger that you may start trying to tempt his appetite. One look from those gorgeous dark eyes is enough to melt your heart, stirring you to greater efforts to find a food that your French Bulldog will really like. At first you may add some gravy, then you may try some chicken . . . The French Bulldog is far from stupid, and he will quickly realize that if he holds out, tastier treats will follow.

This is a bad game to play, because you will quickly run out of tempting delicacies. If your dog is turning up his nose at mealtimes, give him 10 minutes to eat what he wants, and then take up his bowl and give him fresh food at his next meal. Do not feed him treats between meals. If you continue this plan for a couple of days, your French Bulldog will realize that there is nothing to be gained by holding out for better food.

If, however, your dog refuses all food for more than 24 hours, you need to observe his behavior to see if there are any signs of ill health, which may require a trip to the veterinarian. Puppies, especially, need to eat often and can fade very quickly, so be vigilant.

Regurgitation

Some French Bulldogs may regurgitate their food undigested immediately after eating. Others may gulp down water and then regurgitate. If this happens occasionally, there is no cause for concern, but if it occurs regularly it needs to be investigated by your veterinarian.

There is a risk that regular regurgitation is a sign of a serious condition. However, with French Bulldogs there may be other causes, as well. In many cases, it is a reaction to dry food with a high grain content, and a switch to a more natural diet may solve the problem.

As well as a change of diet, you can try feeding three smaller meals per day. Add a spoonful of plain yogurt and feed from a raised bowl about three inches (7.5 cm) off the floor.

Do not to feed your French Bulldog when he is excited, when he has just had a lot of water, or before or after exercise. In all cases, make sure your French Bulldog is allowed to rest quietly after he has eaten his meal.

Bones and chews

Puppies love to chew, and many adults also enjoy gnawing on a bone. A raw marrow bone is ideal, but make sure it is always given under supervision.

Nylon bones are also a favorite with French Bulldogs. They come in a variety of sizes and flavors, and some have raised nodules that are excellent for keeping teeth clean. Rawhide chews are best avoided; it is all too easy for a French Bulldog to bite off a chunk and swallow it, with the danger of it then causing a blockage.

Ideal weight

To keep your French Bulldog in good health it is necessary to monitor his weight. As a breed, French Bulldogs are not prone to obesity as they are not greedy dogs, but there are always exceptions.

A dog who is carrying too much weight is vulnerable to many health problems. He has a poor quality of life because he cannot exercise properly, and he will almost certainly have a reduced life expectancy.

The French Bulldog's close-fitting coat makes it fairly easy to assess his condition. When looking at your dog from above, you should be able to see a definite "waist." You should be able to feel his ribs but not see them.

To keep a check on your dog's weight, get into the habit of visiting your vet clinic once a month just to weigh your dog. You can keep a record and adjust his diet, if necessary. If you are concerned that your French Bulldog is putting on too much weight, or if you think he is underweight, consult your veterinarian, who will help you plan a suitable diet.

Chapter 6

Caring for Your French Bulldog

The French Bulldog is a low-maintenance breed, but that does not mean he doesn't need care. Like all dogs, routine care is important for your Frenchie's health and well-being.

Coat care

With her short coat, a French Bulldog needs minimal grooming—and a puppy requires even less—but do not make the mistake of ignoring this entirely. A grooming session gives you the opportunity to check your dog and discover any minor problems, such as sore spots, or any abnormalities, such as lumps and bumps, which may need to be investigated. Remember, if you spot a problem early on, early diagnosis increases the chances of successful treatment.

The first step is to get your puppy used to being handled so that she willingly accepts the attention. Initially, she will wriggle and attempt to mouth you, but just ignore this. Hold her steady for a few seconds, and reward her when she is still. A puppy needs to learn

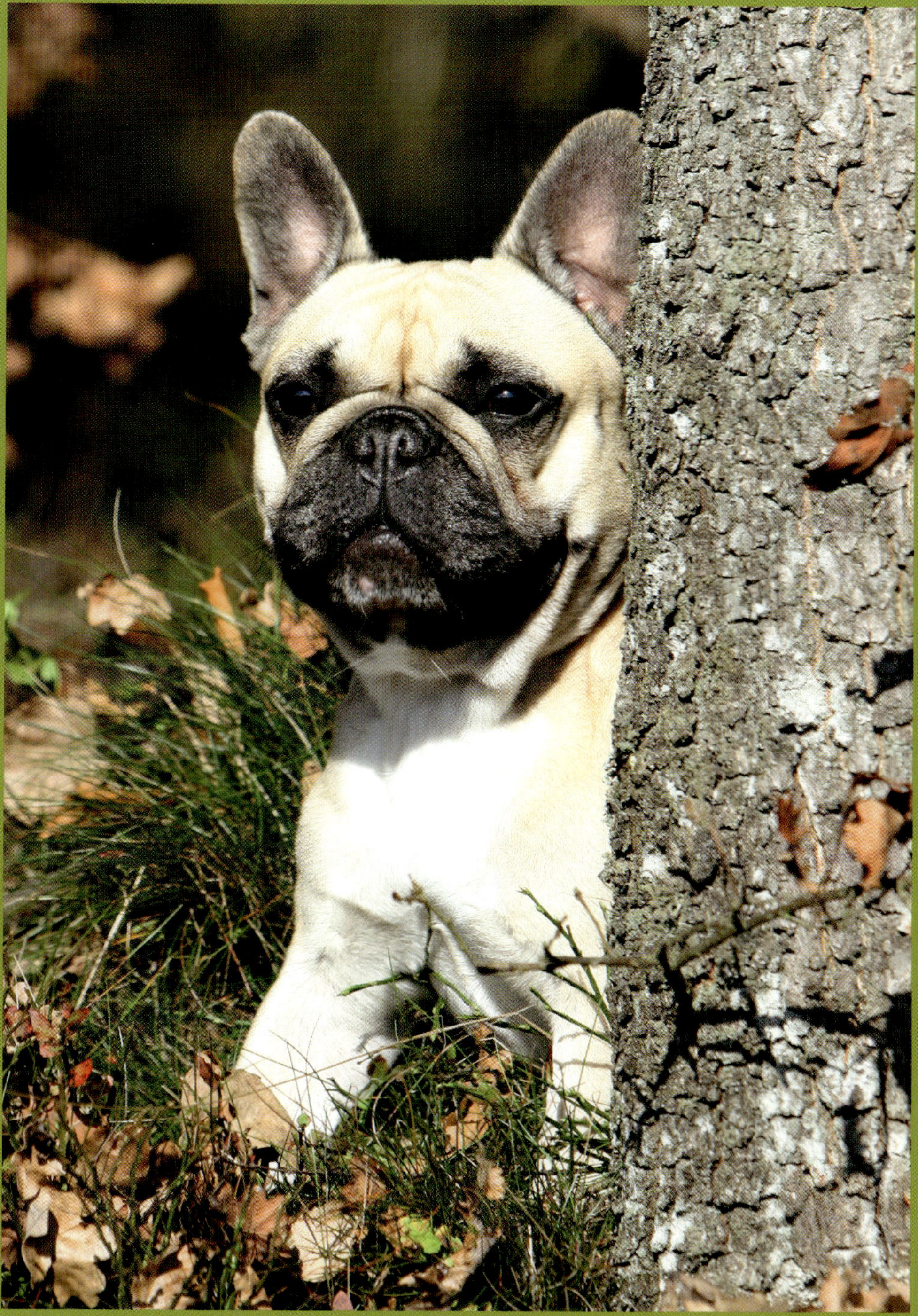

that it is okay to be touched all over; if you fail to do this, she may try to warn you off by growling, which could develop into more problematic behavior.

Start by handling your puppy all over, stroking her from her head to her tail. Lift up each paw in turn, and reward her with a treat when she cooperates. Then roll her over on to her back and tickle her tummy; this is a very vulnerable position for a dog to adopt, so do not force the issue. Be gentle, and give your French Bulldog lots of praise when she does as you ask.

When your French Bulldog is happy to be handled in this way, you can introduce a soft brush and spend a few minutes brushing her coat, and then reward her. She will gradually learn to accept the attention, and will relax while you groom her.

When the adult coat comes in it will be short and smooth with a fine texture. A French Bulldog specialty is the lustrous sheen on a well-groomed, healthy dog. There is no undercoat.

To keep the coat healthy, a quick brush every day is all that is required. A rubber brush or a hound brush work best, as they remove both dirt and dead hair from the coat. If you want your French Bulldog to look really smart, or if you are taking her into the show ring, a rubdown with a chamois leather will bring out the sheen in her coat.

Bathing

A French Bulldog should not be bathed too frequently, as it dries out the skin's natural oils. Not only does this result in a dull coat, but it can also cause dry, itchy skin. Most owners find that a bath every 8 to 12 weeks is enough, unless the dog has found something particularly revolting to roll in!

Make sure you use a mild moisturizing shampoo specially formulated for dogs. You can also use a canine coat conditioner, which will improve the quality and appearance of the coat.

It is a good idea to plan the first bath while your French Bulldog is still small enough to handle easily. She will then become accustomed to the procedure and bathtime will not be a battle.

Routine care

In addition to grooming, your dog needs some routine care. Pay special attention to her face, which must be wiped every day.

Eyes

Check the eyes for signs of soreness or discharge. You can use a piece of cotton—a separate piece for each eye—and wipe away any debris. Remember to be gentle, and reward your dog for cooperating. This should feel like loving care, not an assault.

Ears

The ears should be clean and free from odor. You can buy specially manufactured ear wipes, or you can use a piece of cotton to clean

Grooming

Reward your puppy for standing quietly on the grooming table.

The ears can be a sensitive area, so be gentle when you examine them.

Pick up each paw in turn.

them if necessary. Do not probe into the ear canal or you risk doing more harm than good.

Teeth

Dental disease is becoming more prevalent among dogs, so teeth cleaning should be an essential part of your care regime. The build-up of tartar on the teeth can result in tooth decay, gum infection, and bad breath, and if it is allowed to accumulate, you may have no option but to get the teeth cleaned under anesthesia by a veterinarian.

When your French Bulldog is still a puppy, accustom her to teeth cleaning so it becomes a matter of routine.

Dog toothpaste comes in a variety of meaty flavors that your French Bulldog will like, so you can start by putting some toothpaste on your finger and gently rubbing her teeth. You can then progress to using a finger brush or a toothbrush, whichever you find most convenient.

Remember to reward your French Bulldog when she cooperates and end the session with a fun game. She will positively look forward to her teeth-cleaning sessions.

Tooth brushing demonstration.

Nails

Nail trimming is a task dreaded by many owners, and many dogs, but if you start early on, your French Bulldog will get used to it and will not fight about it.

If your dog has white nails, you will be able to see the quick (the vein and nerves that run through the nail), which you must avoid at all costs. If you cut the quick it will bleed profusely and cause considerable discomfort. Obviously, the task is much harder in dogs with dark nails because you cannot see the quick. The best policy is to trim little and often so the nails don't grow too long, and you do not risk cutting too much and nicking the quick.

If you are worried about trimming your French Bulldog's nails, go to your veterinarian so you can see it done properly. If you are still concerned, you can always use the services of a professional groomer.

Wrinkles

It is absolutely essential that you wipe your French Bulldog's facial wrinkles every day. If you don't, an infection can develop in the crevices, causing painful and unsightly sores.

To clean the wrinkles, take a wad of cotton soaked in lukewarm water, or you can use an unscented wet wipe. Gently wipe along the length of the wrinkles, then dry thoroughly with a clean, dry piece of cotton or a soft towel. (Don't use paper towels, which are rough and will leave behind paper residue.) You can then apply a little petroleum jelly.

Exercise

The French Bulldog thrives on having a busy, interesting life, but she does not need a great deal of exercise. It is important to keep her fit and active. She will enjoy the opportunity to go to many different places and use her nose to explore, but she will generally take things at an easy pace, with an occasional burst of speed for fun.

As a brachycephalic breed, the French Bulldog's respiratory system is not as efficient as it is in other breeds with a more conventional head structure. This means she can overheat very easily, and she can quickly become distressed. For this reason, you should never exercise your French Bulldog in warm weather, and if you are playing a game such as fetch, where she is running (or jogging), stop the game before her breathing becomes labored.

Digestive problems can be linked with exercise, so make sure you wait at least one hour before and after feeding before you exercise your French Bulldog.

The older French Bulldog

We are fortunate that the Frenchie has a pretty good life expectancy—generally around 12 years, and many do slightly better.

As your French Bulldog grows older, she may sleep more and she may be reluctant to go for longer walks. She may show signs of stiffness when she gets up from her bed, but these generally ease when she starts moving.

Some older French Bulldogs may have impaired vision, and some may become a little deaf, but as long as their senses do not deteriorate dramatically, this is something older dogs learn to live with.

If you treat your older dog with kindness and consideration, she will enjoy her later years and suffer the minimum of discomfort.

It is advisable to switch her over to a senior diet, which is more suited to her needs. You may need to adjust the quantity, because she will not be burning up as many calories as she did when she was younger and more energetic. The older French Bulldog will often prefer a softer diet, and you will need to keep a close check on her teeth, as these may cause problems.

Make sure her sleeping quarters are warm and free from drafts, and if she gets wet, be sure to dry her thoroughly.

Most important of all, be guided by your French Bulldog. She will have good days when she feels up to going for a walk, and other days when she would prefer to putter around at home.

Letting go

Inevitably there comes a time when your French Bulldog is not enjoying a good quality of life, and you need to make the painful decision to let her go. We all wish that our dogs died painlessly in their sleep, but unfortunately, this is rarely the case.

However, we can allow our dogs to die with dignity, and to suffer as little as possible, and this should be our way of saying thank you for the wonderful companionship they have given us.

When you feel the time is drawing near, talk to your veterinarian, who will be able to make an objective assessment of your French Bulldog's condition and will help you to make the right decision.

This is the hardest thing you will ever have to do as a dog owner, and it is only natural to grieve for your beloved French Bulldog. But eventually you will be able to look back on the happy memories of times spent together, and this will bring much comfort.

You may, in time, feel that your life is not complete without a French Bulldog, and you will feel ready to welcome a new dog into your home.

Chapter 7

Training Your French Bulldog

To live in the modern world without fear and anxieties, a French Bulldog needs an education in social skills, so that he learns to cope calmly and confidently in a wide variety of situations. The French Bulldog is an outgoing dog with few hang-ups, and will relish the opportunity to broaden his horizons.

Early learning

The breeder will have begun a program of socialization by getting the puppies used to all the sights and sounds of a busy household. You need to continue this when your pup arrives in his new home, making sure he is not worried by household appliances, such as the vacuum cleaner and the washing machine, and that he gets used to unexpected noises from the stereo and television.

It is important to handle your puppy regularly so he will accept grooming and other routine care, and will not be worried if he has to be examined by the veterinarian.

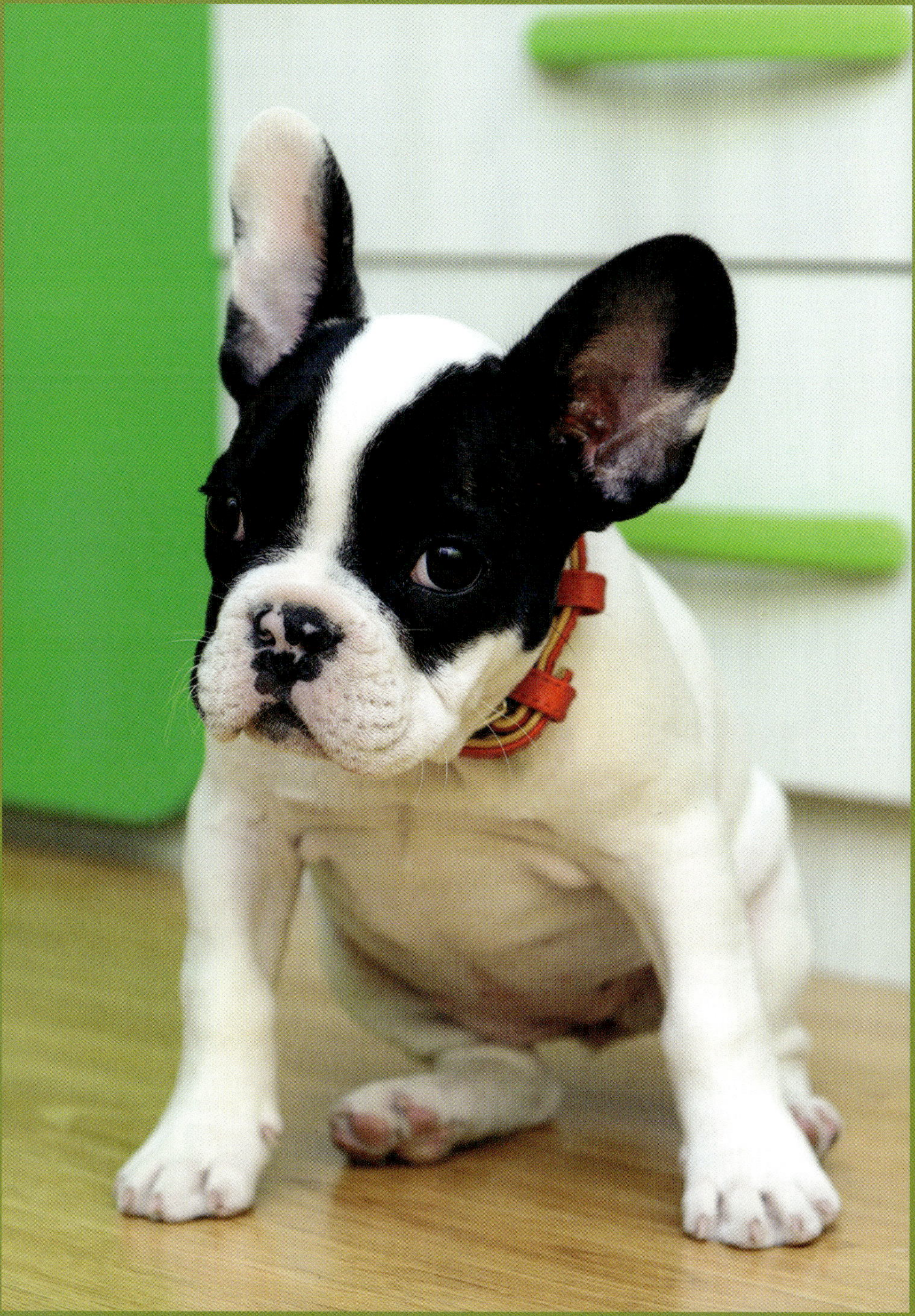

To begin with, your puppy needs to get used to all the members of his new family, but then you should give him the opportunity to meet friends and other people who come to the house.

If you do not have children of your own, make sure your puppy has the chance to meet and play with other people's children—making sure interactions are always supervised—so he learns that humans come in small sizes too.

The French Bulldog is a sociable dog and enjoys the comings and goings of a busy household, so meeting and greeting will rarely be a problem. However, he can be pushy when it comes to getting attention, and although you may feel flattered because your French Bulldog is so focused on you, this behavior needs to be nipped in the bud. The intelligent French Bulldog can be quite manipulative, and will soon get into the habit of demanding attention from you, rather than waiting and asking politely. This is most likely to occur in multidog households, but it can also apply to single dogs.

If you think your French Bulldog is attempting to dictate when and how much attention he gets, adopt the following strategy:

When your French Bulldog jumps up at you, demanding attention (possibly pushing other dogs out of the way), simply ignore him. Turn away and do not speak to him, not even to correct him, as he will regard this as another form of attention. Wait until he is calm and quiet, with all four feet in the ground, and then give him the attention he craves. You will need to be completely consistent in your training and repeat this lesson continually so that your French Bulldog learns that his attention-seeking strategies do not work. He will only get attention when he is calm and you are ready to give it.

If you live in a multidog household, feed your dogs in the same order every time, and when you go for a walk always put leashes on in the same order. The pushy dog must never be first; he has to learn to wait his turn.

This may seem harsh, and the French Bulldog is so appealing it is easy to give in to him. But to live contentedly under the same roof, a French Bulldog must cooperate with all members of his family—human and canine.

The outside world

When your puppy has completed his vaccinations, he is ready to venture into the wider world. As a breed, the French Bulldog is generally confident and self-assured, but there is a lot for a youngster to take in, so do not swamp him with too many new experiences when you first set out.

And of course, you need to work on leash training before you go on your first expedition. There will be plenty of distractions to deal with, so you do not want additional problems of coping with a dog who is pulling or lagging on the leash. Spend some time training, and you can set off with your French Bulldog walking by your side on a loose leash.

He may need additional encouragement when you venture farther afield, so arm yourself with some extra special treats, which will give him a good reason to focus on you when you need him to.

Start by walking your puppy in a quiet area with light traffic, and only progress to a busier place when he is ready. There is so much to see and hear—people (maybe carrying bags or umbrellas), strollers, bicycles, cars, trucks, machinery—so give your puppy a chance to take it all in.

If he does appear worried, do not fall into the trap of sympathizing with him, or worse still, picking him up. This will only teach your pup that he had a good reason to be worried and, with luck, you will "rescue" him if he feels scared.

Instead, give him a little space so he does not have to confront whatever he is frightened of, and distract him with a few treats. Then ask him to walk past, using an encouraging tone of voice, never forcing him by yanking on the leash. Reward him for any forward movement, and your puppy will soon learn that he can trust you and there is nothing to fear.

The French Bulldog is nearly always friendly in his intentions, but other dogs sometimes find it hard to read his body language. Facial expressions in brachycephalic breeds can be more limited, and the French Bulldog does not have a long enough tail to signal his intentions. If you have a friend who has a dog of sound temperament, this is an ideal way to get your puppy used to canine social interactions. As he gets older, you can widen his circle of canine acquaintances.

Training classes

A training class will give your French Bulldog the opportunity to work alongside other dogs in a controlled situation, and he will also learn to focus on you in a different, distracting environment. Both these lessons will be vital as your dog matures.

However, the training class needs to be well run, or you risk doing more harm than good. Before you go along with your puppy, attend a class as an observer to make sure you are happy with what goes on. Find out:

- How much training experience do the instructors have?
- Are the classes divided into appropriate age and size categories?
- Do they use positive, reward-based training methods?
- Do any of the instructors have experience with Frenchies?

If the training class is well run, it is certainly worth attending. Both you and your Frenchie will learn useful training exercises. It will increase his social skills, and you will have the chance to talk to lots of like-minded dog lovers.

Training guidelines

The French Bulldog is a clever dog and is quick to learn. However, he has an independent streak, which means that he may, on occasion, become more focused on following his own agenda than on yours. This is part of his nature, so just be patient and consistent and reward the behaviors you want to see.

You will be keen to get started, but in your rush to get training underway, do not forget the fundamentals that could make the difference between success and failure. You need to get into the mindset of a French Bulldog, figuring out what motivates him and, equally, what makes him switch off. Decide on your priorities for training, set realistic goals, and then think of ways to make your training positive and rewarding.

When you start training, try to observe the following guidelines:

- Choose an area that is free from distractions so your puppy will focus on you. You can progress to a more challenging environment as your pup progresses.
- Do not train your puppy just after he has eaten or exercised. He will either be too full, or too tired, to concentrate.
- Do not train if you are in a bad mood, or if you are short of time—these sessions always end in disaster!
- Providing a worthwhile reward is an essential tool in training. You will probably get the best results if you use some extra special food treats, although some French Bulldogs get very focused on toys, and will see a game with a favorite toy as a top reward.
- If you decide to use a toy, make sure it is only brought out for training sessions, so it accrues added value.
- Keep your verbal cues simple, and always use the same one for each exercise. For example, when you ask your puppy to go into the Down position, the cue is "Down," not "Lie Down," "Get Down," or anything else. Remember, your Frenchie does not speak English; he associates the sound of the word with the action.
- If your dog is finding an exercise difficult, break it down into smaller steps so it is easier to understand.
- Do not make your training sessions boring and repetitious. If training is dull, your puppy will lose focus and go off to find something more interesting to do.
- Do not train for too long, particularly with a young puppy, who has a very short attention span.
- Always end training sessions on a positive note. This does not necessarily mean getting an exercise right. If your pup is

tired and making mistakes, ask him to do a simple exercise so you have the opportunity to praise and reward him. You may find that he benefits from having a break and will make better progress next time you try.

First lessons

Like all puppies, a young French Bulldog will soak up new experiences like a sponge, so training should start from the time your pup arrives in his new home.

Wearing a collar

You may or may not want your French Bulldog to wear a collar all the time. But when he goes out in public places he will need to be on a leash, and so he should be used to the feel of a collar around his neck. Some puppies think nothing of wearing a collar, while others act as if they are being strangled! It is best to accustom your pup to wearing a soft collar for a few minutes at a time, until he gets used to it.

Fit the collar so that you can get at least two fingers between the collar and his neck. Then have a game to distract his attention. This will work for a few moments. Then he will stop and start scratching away at the peculiar thing around his neck. Bend down, rotate the collar, pat him on the head, and distract him by playing with a toy or giving him a treat.

After he has worn the collar for a few minutes each day, he will soon ignore it. Remember, never leave the collar on the puppy unsupervised, especially when he is outside in the yard, or when he is in his crate, as it could get snagged, causing serious injury.

Walking on a leash

This is a simple exercise, but the French Bulldog is surprisingly strong for his size, so it is a good idea to master the basics and for your French Bulldog to learn good leash-walking manners before pulling problems arise.

Once your puppy is used to the collar, take him outside into a secure area, such as your backyard, where there are no distractions. Attach the leash and, to begin with, allow him to wander with the leash trailing, making sure it does not become snagged. Then pick up the leash and follow the pup where he wants to go; he needs to get used to the sensation of being attached to you.

The next stage is to get your Frenchie to follow you, and for this you will need some treats. To give yourself the best chance of success, make sure the treats are high value, so your French Bulldog is motivated to work with you.

Show him you have a treat in your hand, and then encourage him to follow you. Walk a few paces, and if he is walking with you, stop and reward him. If he puts on the brakes, simply change direction and lure him with the treat.

Some French Bulldogs have a hard time understanding that they should not pull on the leash, and in no time, the dog is taking you for a walk. This soon becomes an unpleasant experience, so it is important to make sure your French Bulldog realizes there is absolutely nothing to be gained by pulling.

Begin in an environment that is free from distractions. Walk a few paces, being very aware of any tension on the leash. If you feel the leash tighten and your French Bulldog is attempting to get ahead of you, stop, change direction, and set off again. Your French Bulldog needs to understand that pulling ahead means he doesn't get to go anywhere at all.

Keep a good supply of tasty treats, and remember only reward—with food and verbal praise—when he is walking on a loose leash by your side. The mistake made by many owners at this stage is to use the treats to lure the dog into position, rather than rewarding him for the correct behavior.

Next, introduce some changes of direction so your puppy is walking confidently alongside you. At this stage, introduce the verbal cue "Heel" when your puppy is in the correct position. You can then graduate to walking your puppy away from home, starting in quiet areas and building up to busier environments.

Do not expect too much of your puppy too soon when you are leash walking away from home. He will be distracted by all the new sights and sounds, so concentrating on leash training will be difficult for him. Give him a chance to look and see, and reward him frequently when he is walking forward confidently on a loose leash.

Training tips

Come when called

The French Bulldog is utterly devoted to his family, but there are times when he gets distracted. There are so many enticing smells, places to explore, people and dogs to meet.

He will never stray too far away, but he may not always come back when you ask. The French Bulldog is not a disobedient dog, but recall training can become a real issue; so much so that some French Bulldog owners do not allow their dogs off-leash exercise. This has negative effects on your dog's quality of life, both in terms of restricting his exercise and in denying him the mental stimulation he gets from investigating new places.

Your aim must be to make coming when called even more rewarding than your French Bulldog's personal agenda. This needs to be built up over time, with lots of repetition, so your French Bulldog sees you as a fun person who is always ready to reward him, rather than as an irate owner who is trying to spoil his fun.

Hopefully, the breeder will have started this lesson by calling the puppies to "Come" when it is dinnertime, or when they are moving from one place to another. You can build on this when your puppy arrives in your home, calling him to "Come" when he is in a confined space, such as the kitchen. This is a good place to build up a positive association with the verbal cue—particularly if you ask your puppy to "Come" to get his dinner!

The next stage is to transfer the lesson to a secure outdoor space, such as your backyard. Arm yourself with some treats, and wait until your puppy is distracted. Then call him, using a higher-pitched, excited tone of voice. At this stage, a puppy wants to be with you, so capitalize on this and keep practicing the verbal cue, and rewarding your puppy with a treat and lots of praise when he comes, so he knows it is worth his while to come to you.

Now you are ready to introduce some distractions. Try calling him when someone else is in the yard, or wait a few minutes until he is investigating a really interesting scent. If your puppy responds, immediately reward him with a treat. If he is slow to come, run away a few steps and then call again, making yourself sound really exciting. Jump up and down, open your arms wide to welcome him; it doesn't matter how silly you look, he needs to see you as the most fun person in the world.

When you have a reliable recall in the yard, you can venture into the outside world. Do not be too ambitious to begin with; try a recall in a quiet place with a minimum of distractions so you can be assured of success.

Do not make the mistake of asking your dog to come only at the end of his off-leash exercise or time in the yard. What is the incentive in coming back to you if all you do is clip on his leash, marking the end of his free time? Instead, call your dog at random times, giving him a treat and a pat, and then letting him go free again. This way, he learns that coming to you—and focusing on you—is always rewarding.

Stationary exercises

The Sit and Down are easy to teach, and mastering these exercises will be rewarding for both you and your French Bulldog. The Frenchie can be quite excitable, so it is useful to have a way of quickly settling him before everyone gets carried away!

Sit

The best way to teach this cue is to lure your French Bulldog into position, and for this you can use a treat or his food bowl as the reward. Hold the reward above his head and move it slightly back. As he looks up, he will lower his hindquarters and go into a sit.

Practice this a few times, and when your puppy understands what the exercise is about, introduce the verbal cue, "Sit."

When your Frenchie understands the exercise, he will respond to the verbal cue alone, and you will not need to lure or even reward him every time he sits. However, it is a good idea to give him treats at random times when he cooperates, to keep him guessing! And always reward him with praise, so he knows he's made the right choice.

Down

This is an important lesson, and can be a lifesaver if an emergency arises and you need to bring your Frenchie to an instant halt.

This is an easier exercise to teach if you start with your dog in a Sit. Stand or kneel in front of him and show him you have a treat in your hand. Hold the treat just in front of his nose and slowly lower it toward the ground, between his front legs. As your French Bulldog follows the treat, he will go down on his front legs and, in a few moments, his hindquarters will follow.

Close your hand over the treat so he doesn't cheat and get the treat before he is in the correct position. As soon as he is all the way Down, give him the treat and lots of praise. Keep practicing, and when your Frenchie understands what you want, introduce the verbal cue "Down."

Clicker Training

There are many different methods of training, and as long as the methods you use are positive and reward-based, you will not go wrong.

You may decide you want to try clicker training—a modern approach that has proved very effective. The clicker is the size of a matchbox, fitted with a small device that makes a clicking noise when it is pressed. The dog is taught that a click means a reward will follow, so he quickly learns to work for a click. The benefit is that the click enables us to precisely mark the behavior we are trying to elicit. Then, even if we're slow with the treat, the message has been delivered.

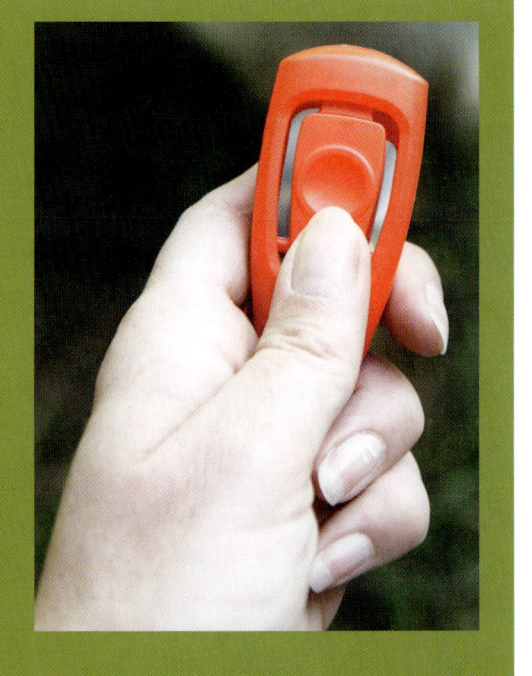

As a trainer, you need to get your timing right and click at the precise moment your dog does what you want, then reward him. This way, your dog will repeat the desired behavior, knowing that he will earn a click and then get a treat. Clicker training is easy with puppies, and adult dogs too.

Control exercises

Dogs do not always find self-control easy, and these exercises are not the most exciting. But they will make your dog much easier to live with. And he will understand that he will be rewarded for cooperating with you.

Wait

This exercise teaches your French Bulldog to wait in position until you give him another cue. It differs from the Stay exercise, where he must stay where you have left him for a longer period.

The most useful application of "Wait" is when you are walking him and need him to wait at the curb, or are getting your dog out of the car and you need him to stay in position until you clip on his leash.

Start with your puppy on the leash to give you a greater chance of success. Ask him to "Sit," then stand at his side. Take one step forward and hold your hand back behind you, palm facing the dog. Step back, release him with a word, such as "Okay," and then reward him.

Practice this a few times, waiting a little longer before you reward him, and then introduce the verbal cue "Wait." You can reinforce the lesson by using it in different situations, such as asking your Frenchie to "Wait" before you put his food bowl down.

Stay

You need to differentiate this exercise from the Wait by using a different hand signal and a different verbal cue.

Start with your French Bulldog in the Down, as he is most likely to be secure in this position. Face him and take one step back, holding your hand, palm flat, facing him. Wait a second and then come back to stand in front of him.

Practice until your Frenchie understands the exercise, and then introduce the verbal cue "Stay." Gradually increase the distance between you and your puppy, and increase the challenge by walking around him—and even stepping over him—so that he learns he must "Stay" until you release him, using your release word, "Okay."

Leave

A response to this verbal cue means your French Bulldog will learn to give up a toy on request, and it follows that he will give up anything when he is asked, which is very useful if he has got hold of a forbidden object such as a shoe or somebody's glove.

This is particularly important with a Frenchie, who can become possessive with favorite toys or places of high value, such as the sofa, or even your bed!

The "Leave" command can be taught quite easily when you are first playing with your puppy. As you gently take a toy from his mouth, introduce the verbal cue, "Leave," and then praise him. If he is reluctant, swap the toy for another toy or a treat. This will usually do the trick.

Do not try to pull the toy from his mouth if he refuses to give it up, as you will make the situation confrontational. Let the toy go "dead" in your hand, and then swap it for a new toy, or a really high-value treat, so this becomes the better option.

Remember to make a big fuss over your French Bulldog when he does as you ask, so he learns that cooperation is always the best—and most rewarding—option.

Again, the strategy is not to be confrontational but to offer him a better reward, such as a treat or a toy, and then call him to you. As far as the Frenchie is concerned, he has not been forced to give up the thing he values; he has simply been offered something better—a win-win situation!

Chapter 8

Keeping Your Frenchie Busy

The French Bulldog is an intelligent and adaptable dog, but there are limitations when it comes to competing in some of the canine sports.

Few Frenchies (or their owners!) have an appetite for rigorous training, and most get bored very quickly if they are asked to do something too often. The best plan is to focus on having fun with your French Bulldog—and who knows, you may even surprise yourselves.

Canine Good Citizen

The American Kennel Club runs the Canine Good Citizen program. It promotes responsible ownership and helps you to train a well-behaved dog who will fit in with the community.

The program tests your dog on basic good manners, alone and with other people and dogs around. It's excellent for all pet owners

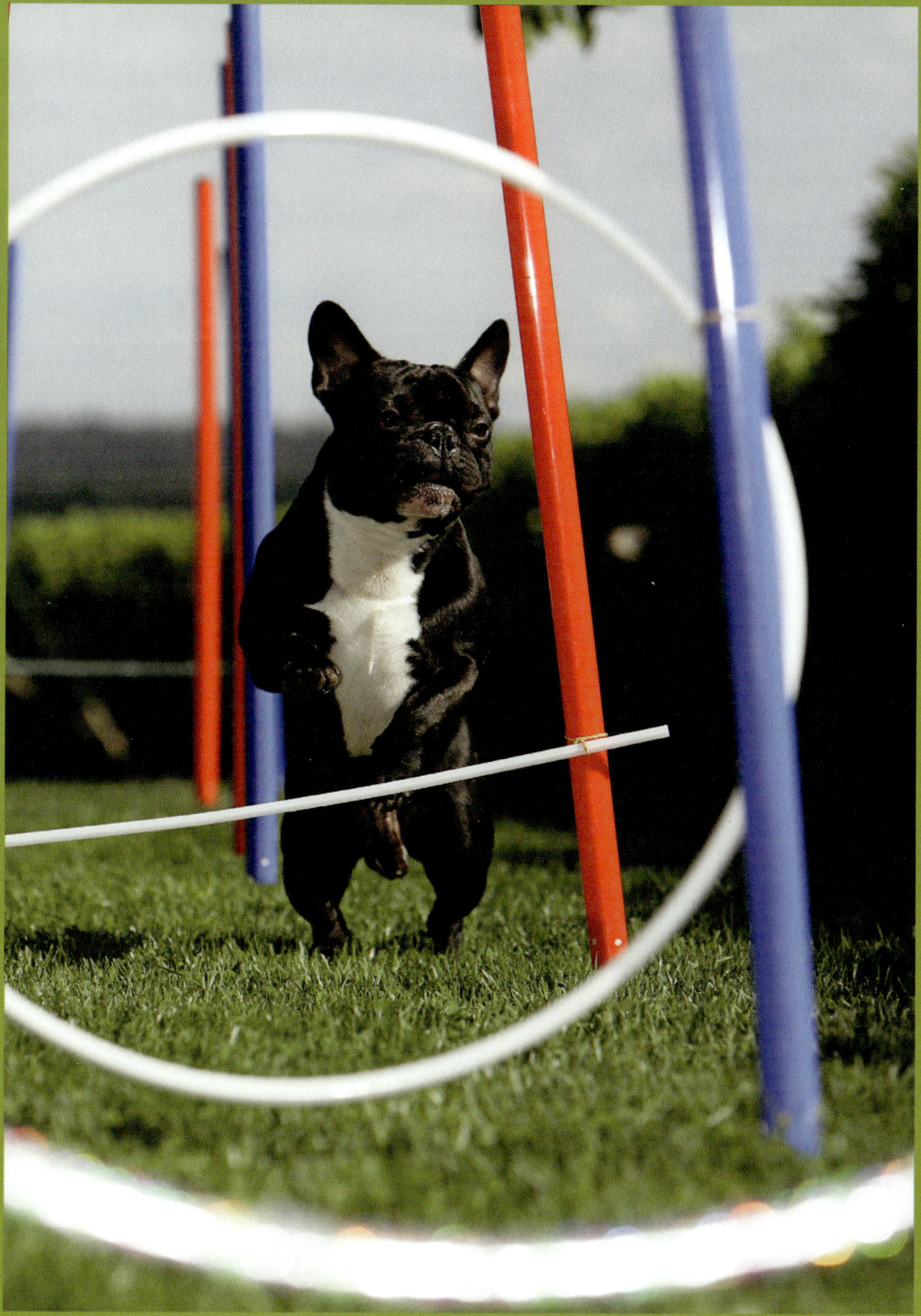

and is also an ideal starting point if you plan to compete with your Frenchie in any sport.

Obedience

If your French Bulldog has mastered the basic exercises for the Canine Good Citizen program, you may want to get involved in competitive obedience.

Competitive obedience exercises include: heel work at varying paces with dog and handler following a pattern decided by the judge, stays, recalls, retrieves, send-aways, scent discrimination, and distance control. The exercises get progressively harder as you rise in the classes. A French Bulldog will readily learn these exercises, but this is a discipline that calls for a very high degree of precision and accuracy, which does not suit all dogs—or all handlers.

Rally O

If you do not want to get involved in the rigors of competitive obedience, you may find that a sport called Rally O is more to your liking. This is loosely based on obedience, and also has a few exercises borrowed from agility when you get to the highest levels. Handler and dog must complete a course, in the designated order, that has anywhere from 12 to 20 exercises. The course is timed and the team must finish within the time limit, but there are no bonus points for speed.

The great advantage of Rally O is that it is very relaxed, and anyone can compete; indeed, it has proved very popular for handlers with disabilities, because they are able to work their dogs to a high standard and compete on equal terms.

Agility

The French Bulldog is small and powerful and she should also be active, so agility is a sport worth considering—even though you are unlikely to win the medals here, going up against more athletic breeds.

Agility is basically a canine obstacle course. The obstacles include hurdles, long jump, tire jump, tunnels (rigid and collapsible), weaving poles, an A-frame, a dog-walk, and a seesaw. You'll need a good element of control, because dogs compete off-leash.

Agility is judged on the time taken to get around the course, with faults given for knocking down fences, missing obstacles, and going through the course in the wrong order.

Puppies should not be allowed to do any agility exercises that

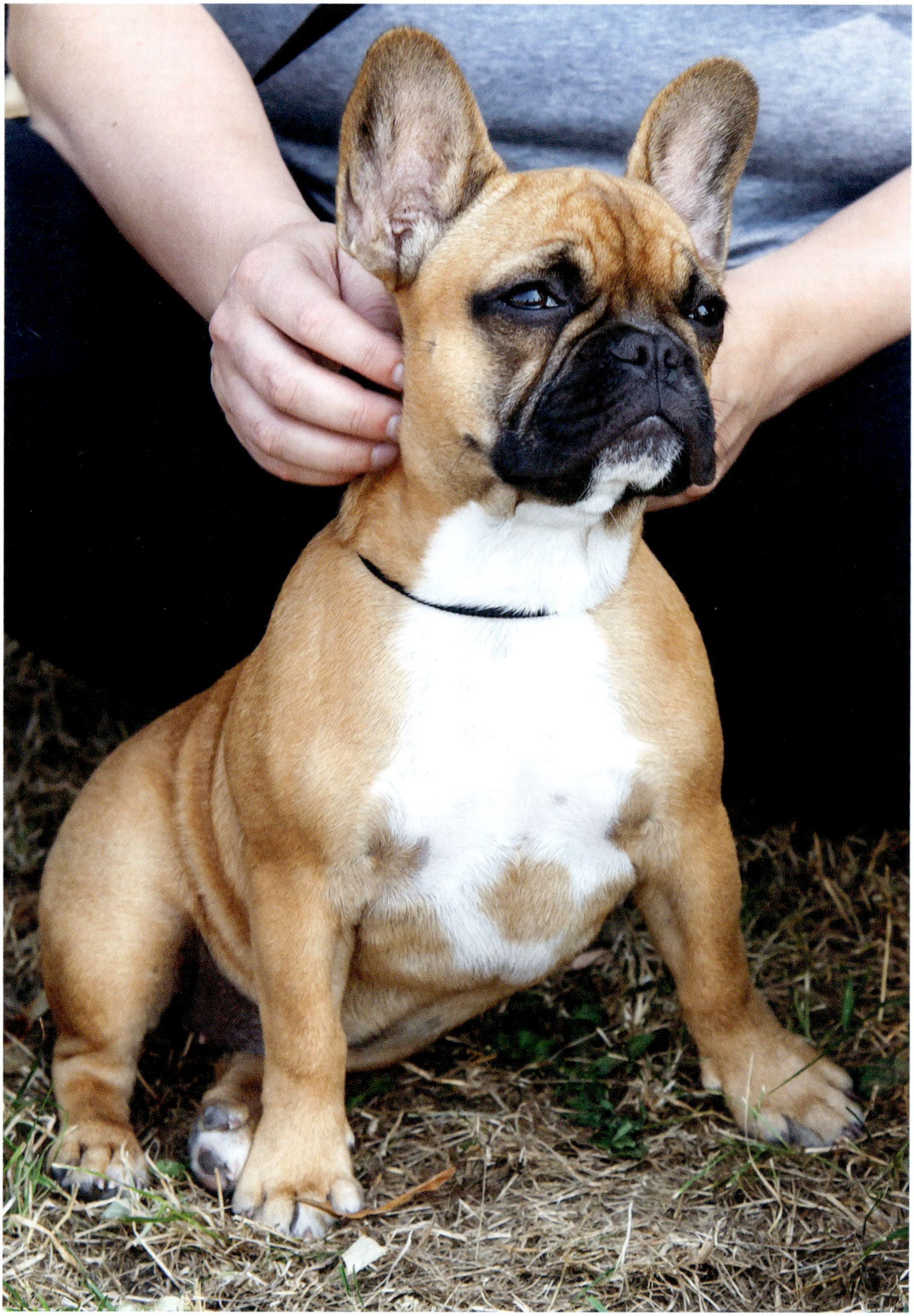

involve jumping or contact equipment until at least 12 months old. But while you are waiting, you can begin to teach your dog how to weave, introduce her to tunnels, and play around the jumps and poles so that she becomes familiar with the equipment.

Musical freestyle

This is a relatively new discipline that is growing in popularity. Dog and handler must perform a choreographed routine to music, allowing the dog to perform an array of tricks and moves that delight the crowd.

There are two categories: freestyle heeling, where the dog stays close to her handler in a variety of positions; and canine freestyle, where the dog works at a greater distance and performs some of the more spectacular moves. A panel of judges marks the routine for choreography, accuracy, and musical interpretation. Both categories demand a huge amount of training, but if you keep training sessions lighthearted, with plenty of positive reinforcement, the French Bulldog will prove to be a real crowd pleaser!

Showing

Exhibiting a dog in the show ring sounds easy, but in fact, it entails a lot of training and preparation, particularly when you are asking a strong-minded breed to compete in a dog show.

Your French Bulldog will have to be calm and confident in the busy show atmosphere, so you need to work on her socialization, and also take her to ringcraft classes so you can both learn what is required in the ring. Your French Bulldog will be subjected to a detailed hands-on examination by the judge. She must also learn to stand still in a show pose and to move on a loose leash so the judge can assess her gait. Showing at the top level is highly addictive and highly competitive, so you will need to learn the art of winning—and losing—graciously.

Chapter 9

Health Care

With routine care, a well-balanced diet, and sufficient exercise, most dogs will experience few health problems. However, it is your responsibility to put a program of preventive health care in place—and this should start from the moment your puppy, or adult dog, arrives in his new home.

Parasites

No matter how well you look after your Frenchie, you will have to accept that parasites—internal and external—are ever present, and you need to take preventive action.

Internal parasites live inside your dog. These are the various worms. Most will find a home in the digestive tract, but there is also a parasite that lives in the heart. If infestation is unchecked, a dog's health will be severely jeopardized, but routine preventive treatment is simple and effective.

External parasites live on your dog's body—in his skin and fur, and sometimes in his ears.

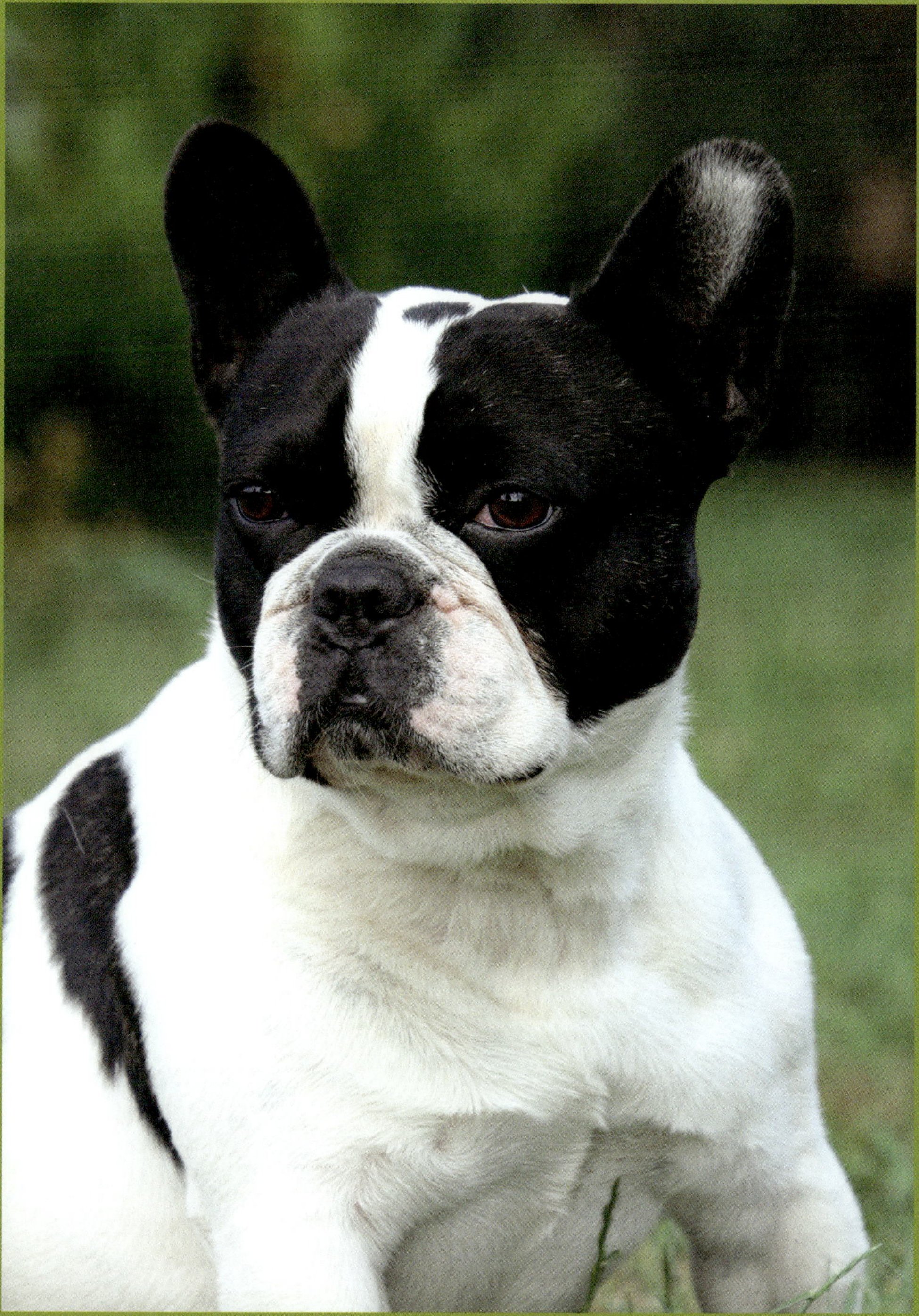

Vaccination Program

The American Animal Hospital Association and the American Veterinary Medical Association have issued vaccination guidelines that apply to all breeds of dogs. They divide the available vaccines into two groups: core vaccines, which every dog should get, and non-core vaccines, which are optional.

Core vaccines are canine parvovirus-2, distemper, and adenovirus-2. Puppies should get vaccinated every three to four weeks between the ages of 6 and 16 weeks, with the final dose at 14 to 16 weeks of age. If a dog older than 16 weeks is getting their first vaccine, one dose is enough. Dogs who received an initial dose at less than 16 weeks should be given a booster after one year, and then every three years or more thereafter.

Rabies is also a core vaccine. For puppies less than 16 weeks old, a single dose should be given no earlier than 12 weeks of age. Revaccination is recommended annually or every three years, depending on the vaccine used and state and local laws.

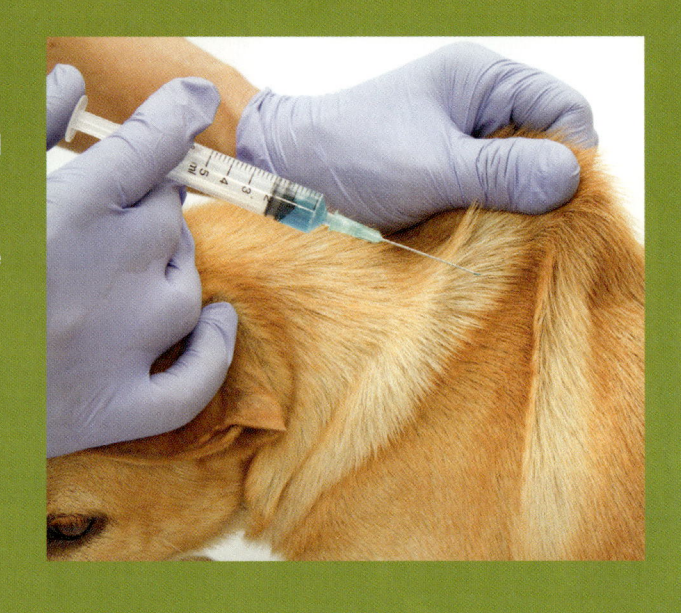

Non-core vaccines are canine parainfluenza virus, Bordetella bronchiseptica, canine influenza virus, canine measles, leptospirosis, and Lyme disease.

The dog's exposure risk, lifestyle, and geographic location all come into play when deciding which non-core vaccines may be appropriate for your dog. Have a conversation with your veterinarian about the right vaccine protocol for your dog.

Roundworm

This is found in the small intestine. Signs of infestation will be a poor coat, a potbelly, diarrhea, and lethargy. Prospective mothers should be treated before mating, but it is almost inevitable that parasites she may have will be passed on to the puppies. For this reason, a breeder will start a worming program, which you will need to continue. Ask your vet for advice on treatment, which will need to continue throughout your dog's life.

Tapeworm

Infection occurs when the dog ingests fleas or lice. The adult worm takes up residence in the small intestine, releasing mobile segments (which contain eggs), which can be seen in a dog's feces as small rice-like grains. The only other obvious sign of infestation is irritation of the anus. Again, routine preventive treatment is required throughout your dog's life.

Heartworm

This parasite is transmitted by mosquitoes, and is found in all parts of the USA, although its prevalence does vary. Heartworms live in the right side of the heart and larvae can grow up to 14 inches (35 cm) long. A dog with heartworm is at severe risk from heart failure, so preventive treatment, as advised by your vet, is essential. Dogs should also have regular tests to check for the presence of infection.

Lungworm

Lungworm is a parasite that lives in the heart and major blood vessels supplying the lungs. It can cause many problems, such as breathing difficulties, excessive bleeding, sickness, diarrhea, seizures, and even death. The dog becomes infected when ingesting slugs and snails, often accidentally when rummaging through undergrowth. Lungworm is not common, but it is on the increase and a responsible owner should be aware of it. Fortunately, it is easily preventable, and even affected dogs usually make a full recovery if treated early enough. Your vet will be able to advise you on the risks in your area and what form of treatment may be required.

Fleas

A dog may carry many types of fleas. The flea stays on the dog only long enough to feed and breed, but its presence will result in itching. If your dog has an allergy to fleas—usually a reaction to the flea's saliva—he will scratch himself until he is raw. Spot-ons and chewable flea preven-

How to Detect Fleas

You may suspect your dog has fleas, but how can you be sure? There are two methods to try. Run a fine comb through your dog's coat, and see if you can detect the presence of fleas on the skin, or clinging to the comb. Alternatively, sit your dog on some white paper and rub his back. This will dislodge feces from the fleas, which will be visible as small brown specks. To double check, shake the specks onto some damp cotton balls. Flea feces consist of the dried blood taken from the host, so if the specks turn a lighter shade of red, you know your dog has fleas.

tives are easy to use and highly effective, and should be given regularly to prevent fleas entirely. Some also prevent ticks.

If your dog has fleas, talk to your veterinarian about the best treatment. Bear in mind that your entire home, dog's whole environment, and all other pets in your home will also need to be treated.

Ticks

These are blood-sucking parasites that are most frequently found in areas where sheep or deer are present. The main danger is their ability to pass a wide variety of very serious diseases—including Lyme disease—to both dogs and humans. The preventive you give your dog for fleas generally works for ticks, but you should discuss the best product to use with your veterinarian.

Ear mites

These parasites live in the outer ear canal. The signs of infestation are a brown, waxy discharge, and your dog will often shake his head and scratch his ear. If you suspect your dog has ear mites, a visit to the vet will be needed so that medicated ear drops can be prescribed.

Cheyletiella mange

These small, white mites are visible to the naked eye and are often referred to as "walking dandruff." They cause a scruffy coat and mild itchiness. They are zoonotic—transferable to humans—so prompt treatment with an insecticide prescribed by your veterinarian is essential.

Chiggers

These are picked up from the undergrowth, and can be seen as bright red, yellow, or orange specks on the webbing between the toes, although this can also be found elsewhere on the body, such as on the ear flaps. Treatment is effective with the appropriate insecticide, prescribed by your vet.

Skin mites

There are two types of parasite that burrow into a dog's skin. Demodex canis is transferred from a mother to her pups while they are feeding. Treatment is with a topical preparation, and sometimes antibiotics are needed. Refer to your vet.

The other skin mite is *sarcoptes scabiei*, which causes intense itching and hair loss. It is highly contagious, so all dogs in a household will need to be treated, which involves repeated baths with a medicated shampoo.

Common ailments

As with all living animals, dogs can be affected by a variety of ailments, most of which can be treated effectively after consulting with your vet, who will prescribe appropriate medication and will advise you on how to care for your dog's needs.

Here are some of the more common problems that could affect your Frenchie, with advice on how to deal with them.

How to Remove a Tick

If you spot a tick on your dog, do not try to pluck it off, as you risk leaving the hard mouth parts embedded in his skin. The best way to remove a tick is to use a pair of fine tweezers, or you can buy a tick remover. Grasp the tick head firmly and then pull the tick straight out from the skin. If you are using a tick remover, check the instructions, as some recommend a circular twist when pulling. When you have removed the tick, clean the area with mild soap and water.

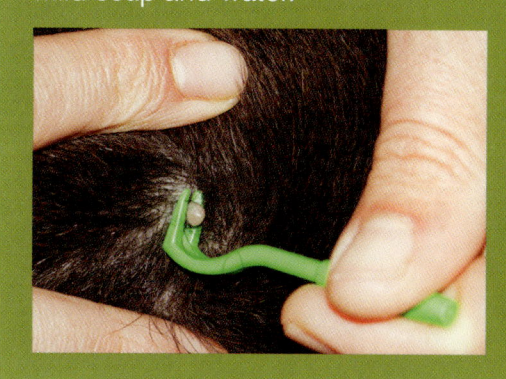

Anal glands

These are two small sacs on either side of the anus, which produce a dark brown secretion. The anal glands should empty every time a dog defecates, but if they become blocked or impacted, a dog will experience increasing discomfort. He may lick at his rear end, or scoot his bottom along the ground to relieve the irritation.

Treatment involves a trip to the vet, who will empty the glands manually. It is important to do this without delay or they could become infected.

Dental problems

Dental problems are becoming increasingly common in dogs, and can cause serious discomfort. Good dental hygiene will do much to minimize problems with gum infection and tooth decay. If tartar accumulates to the extent that you cannot remove it by brushing, your dog will need to be anesthetized for a dental cleaning by the veterinarian.

Diarrhea

There are many reasons why a dog might have diarrhea, but most commonly it is the result of scavenging, a sudden change of diet, or an adverse reaction to a particular type of food.

If your dog is suffering from diarrhea, the first step is to withhold food for a day. It is important that he does not become dehydrated, so make sure fresh drinking water is available. However, drinking too much can increase the diarrhea, which may be accompanied with vomiting, so limit how much he drinks at any one time.

After allowing the stomach to rest, feed a bland diet, such as white fish or chicken with boiled rice for a few days. In most cases, your dog's motions will return to normal and you can resume normal feeding, although this should be done gradually.

However, if this fails to work and the diarrhea persists for more than a few days, you should consult your vet. Your dog may have an infection, which needs to be treated with antibiotics, or the diarrhea may indicate some other problem that needs expert diagnosis.

Ear infections

The French Bulldog has erect ears that allow the air to circulate freely, thus minimizing the risk of ear infections. A healthy ear is clean, with no sign of redness or inflammation, and no evidence of a waxy brown discharge or a foul odor. If you see your dog scratching her ear, shaking her head, or holding one ear at an odd angle, you will need to consult your vet. The most likely causes are ear mites, an infection, or there may a foreign body, such as a grass seed, trapped in the ear.

A vet shows how to clean ears.

Depending on the cause, treatment is with medicated ear drops, possibly containing antibiotics. If a foreign body is suspected, the vet will need to carry out further investigation.

Eye problems

The French Bulldog has round eyes, which should not be sunken nor prominent. This lack of exaggeration means the eyes should not be predisposed to infection or vulnerable to injury or trauma. However, there is a tendency toward more prominent eyes in the breed, and this can lead to problems such as corneal ulcers.

This is generally caused by a cornea irritation. Treatment with eye drops is effective, particularly if administered before the condition deteriorates. In severe cases, surgery may be required.

If your French Bulldog's eyes look red and sore, he may be suffering from conjunctivitis. This may or may not be accompanied by a watery or a crusty discharge. Conjunctivitis can be caused by a bacterial or viral infection, it could be the result of an injury, or it may be a reaction to pollen. Conjunctivitis may also be the first sign of more serious inherited eye problems, which will be discussed later in this chapter.

You will need to consult your veterinarian for a correct diagnosis, but in the case of an infection, treatment with medicated eye drops is effective.

Heatstroke

The French Bulldog has a flat, upturned nose, and although the nostrils should be open to allow for normal breathing, it is inevitable that breathing is more labored in the brachycephalic breeds, and they are therefore more likely to overheat. In its mildest form this causes discomfort, but if a French Bulldog's body temperature rises so that he develops heatstroke, the consequences can be disastrous.

When the temperature rises, make sure your dog always has access to shady areas, and wait for a cooler part of the day before going for a walk. Never leave your dog in the car, as the temperature can rise dramatically—even on a cloudy day. Heatstroke can happen very rapidly, and unless you are able to lower your dog's temperature, it can be fatal.

The signs of heatstroke include heavy panting and difficulty breathing, bright red tongue and mucous membranes, thick saliva, and vomiting. Eventually, the dog becomes progressively unsteady and passes out.

If your dog appears to be suffering from heatstroke, this is a true emergency. Lie him flat and then cool him as quickly as possible by hosing him down or covering him with wet towels. As soon as he has made some recovery, take him to the veterinarian.

Skin problems

The Frenchie can be prone to skin problems, which may cause hair loss, soreness, and itching. Fleas and other external parasites can result in itching, and the skin can become very sore and inflamed if the dog has an allergic reaction. Preventive treatment is obviously essential, but if you suspect an allergic reaction, you may need to seek veterinary advice.

Food intolerance (particularly grain products) and environmental factors, such as dust mites or pollen, can also cause major skin problems. The problem here is finding the cause, and this can only be done by a process of elimination, such as removing specific foods from the diet. Again, you will need help from your veterinarian.

Breed-specific disorders

Like all pedigreed dogs, the French Bulldog does have some breed-related disorders. If your dog is diagnosed with any of the diseases listed here, it is important to remember that they can affect offspring, so it is not wise to breed affected dogs.

There are now recognized screening tests that enable breeders to check for carrier and affected individuals, and hence reduce the prevalence of these diseases within the breed. DNA testing is also becoming more widely available, and as research into genetic diseases progresses, more DNA tests are being developed.

Brachycephalic Syndrome

Brachycephalic breeds, including the French Bulldog, are predisposed to this condition because their physical makeup can lead to defects such as an elongated soft palate, narrowed nostrils, abnormalities of the larynx, and/or a narrow windpipe. Minor signs are snuffling and snorting, progressing to intolerance to exercise and breathing difficulties, with collapse of the larynx in its most severe form. Other symptoms of elongated soft palate are spitting up or regurgitating food or foam frequently.

Guarding against over-exertion and overheating is vital for

all Frenchies, but especially for affected dogs. Surgery, which is high-risk for dogs with this condition, can be used to shorten an elongated soft palate.

Hip dysplasia

In dogs with this structural problem, the ball and socket joint of the hip develops incorrectly so that the head of the femur (ball) and the acetabulum of the pelvis (socket) do not fit snugly. This causes pain in the joint, and may be seen as lameness in dogs as young as five months old, with deterioration into severe arthritis over time. Gentle exercise, keeping the dog at a good weight, anti-inflammatory drugs, and home management are all part of the treatment. Severe cases may require surgery.

Frenchies, like many other breeds, can be affected by hip dysplasia, and all potential breeding animals should therefore be screened by having their hips scored. X-rays are submitted to the Orthopedic Foundation for Animals or PennHIP, where they are graded according to the degree of hip laxity.

Hip dysplasia is thought to have a genetic component, but the mode of inheritance has not been established, since multiple genes are involved. Environmental factors, such as nutrition and rapid growth, may also play a role in its development.

Patellar luxation

This is an orthopedic problem, where the dog's kneecap slips out of place because of anatomical deformities in the joint. Treatment involves rest and anti-inflammatory medications. In more severe cases, surgery may be the best option. The Orthopedic Foundation for Animals (OFA) grades the degree of luxation or certifies that a dog is clear, based on X-rays.

Hemivertebrae

In dogs with this condition, the vertebrae are misshapen or deformed and cannot therefore protect the spinal cord. The effect depends on which vertebrae are affected, varying from kinking of the spinal column, hind limb weakness, or, at worst, paralysis. Surgery may be possible in some cases.

It has been found that puppies with very short bodies are more likely to be affected, and it is essential that all potential breeding animals are thoroughly assessed by X-ray.

Juvenile cataracts

Cataracts cloud the lens of your dog's eyes. They can appear in either or both eyes. Because Frenchies are genetically predisposed to developing cataracts, they can show up in relatively young dogs. Some cataracts are small and do not grow, some grow slowly, but others can render your dog blind in a short time. Because hereditary cataracts can progress quickly, your veterinarian might recommend surgery earlier than they would on a dog with a non-genetically-based cataract. The surgery is complicated and has a relatively long recovery time, but typically an excellent outcome. Companion Animal Eye Registry (CAER) recommends annual testing. There is also a DNA test for the congenital form, which is also known as juvenile cataracts.

Autoimmune thyroiditis

Hypothyroidism, or impaired thyroid gland function with low thyroid hormone levels, is seen in Frenchies. It often develops slowly over several months or years. The dog may be listless, with a poor coat, and often gains weight. This disease is not easy to diagnose, and repeated testing may be necessary. It is treated with thyroid supplements.

Heart problems

Cardiomyopathy is a genetic disease that appears to run in family lines and causes ventricular premature complexes (irregular beats) of the heart in adult dogs. Clinical signs include coughing or breathlessness, exercise intolerance, collapse, and sudden death.

Treatment is aimed at slowing the progression of the disease and controlling the clinical signs with daily medication.

Heart murmurs are abnormal heart sounds heard by stethoscope. A heart murmur is caused by turbulent blood flow within the heart. Heart murmurs can be caused by a structural problem within the heart. To detect these problems, an echocardiogram is necessary.

Summing up

This has been a long list of health problems, but it was not my intention to scare you. Acquiring some basic knowledge is an asset, as it will allow you to spot signs of trouble at an early stage. Early diagnosis very often leads to the most effective treatment.

The Frenchie as a breed is a generally healthy, energetic dog with a zest for life, and annual check-ups will be all he needs. As a companion, he will bring many happy memories in the years you will spend together.

Find Out More

Books

Bradshaw, John. *Dog Sense: How the New Science of Dog Behavior Can Make You a Better Friend to Your Pet*. New York: Basic Books, 2014.

Canova, Ali, Joe Canova, and Diane Godspeed, *Agility Training for You and Your Dog: From Backyard Fun to High-Performance Training*. New York: Lyons Press, 2008.

Eldredge, Debra, DVM, and Kate Eldredge. *Idiot's Guides: Dog Tricks*. New York: Alpha, 2015.

Eldredge, Debra M., DVM, Liisa D. Carlson, DVM, Delbert G. Carlson, DVM, and James M. Giffin, MD. *Dog Owner's Home Veterinary Handbook*. 4th Ed. New York: Howell Book House, 2007.

Stilwell, Victoria. *Train Your Dog Positively: Understand Your Dog and Solve Common Behavior Problems Including Separation Anxiety, Excessive Barking, Aggression, Housetraining, Leash Pulling, and More!* Berkeley: Ten Speed Press, 2013.

Websites

www.akc.org American Kennel Club

fbdca.org French Bull Dog Club of America

www.petmd.com PetMD

www.ukcdogs.com United Kennel Club

Series Glossary of Key Terms

agility   in this case, a canine sport in which dogs navigate an obstacle course

breed standard   a detailed written description of the ideal type, size, shape, colors, movement, and temperament of a dog breed

conforms   aligns with, agrees with

docked   cut or shortened

dysplasia   a structural problem with the joints, when the bones do not fit properly together

heatstroke   a medical condition in which the body overheats to a dangerous degree

muzzle   (n) the nose and mouth of a dog; (v) to place a restraint on the mouth of a dog

neuter   to make a male dog unable to create puppies

parasites   organisms that live and feed on a host organism

pedigree   the formal record of an animal's descent, usually showing it to be purebred

socialization   the process of introducing a dog to as many different sights, sounds, animals, people, and experiences as possible, so he will feel comfortable with them all

spay   to make a female dog unable to create puppies

temperament   the basic nature of an animal, especially as it affects their behavior

Index

adult dogs, 37
agility sports, 107, 109
ailments, 117-121
bathing, 79
beds, 53-54
bones, 73-74
bowls, 56
brachycephalic breeds, 8, 122-123
breed history, 11-15
breed standards
  body shape, 23
  gait, 25
  head, skull, 20
  legs, tail, 24
  mouth, neck, 21
  significance of, 16, 18
  size (weight), 18
breeders, 41-44
bull baiting, 11-12
Canine Good Citizen, 104, 106
cataracts, 124
cats, 63-64
chews, 73-74
chiggers, 116
children, 61-62, 88
clicker training, 100
coat
  breeding new colors, 14-15
  care of, 76, 78-80
  colors and patterns of, 22, 25, 34
  ideal texture of, 24
collars, 54, 95
companion dogs, 26-27
companion puppies, 46-47
control exercises, 100-103
crates, 52-53
dental care, 81
dental problems, 118
diarrhea, 118-119
diets, 69-71
disorders, 121-125

ears
  cleaning, 79-81
  controversy regarding, 12-13
  shape and placement of, 20
  signs of infection in, 119
  signs of mites in, 115-116
English Bulldogs, 11-12
exercise, 83
eyes
  annual exams of, 44-45
  cleaning, 79
  common ailments of, 119-120
  disorders of, 124
  size and color of, 20
family introductions, 60-61
family pets, 62
feeding, 56, 64-65
feeding schedules, 71-73
female dogs, 33-34
fleas, 114-115
French Bulldogs
  adopting multiple, 35, 37
  history of, 13-15
grooming, 76, 78-79
grooming equipment, 57
health issues, 44-45
heart problems, 125
heatstroke, 120-121
hemivertebrae condition, 123-124
hip dysplasia, 44, 123
home safety, 48, 50-51
house rules, 52
household appliances, 86, 88
housetraining, 67-69
identification, 54-55
intelligence, 10, 27
leashes, 54, 95-97
living arrangements, 11
male dogs, 33-34
mange, 116
mental stimulation, 32
microchips, 54-55
musical freestyle, 109

nail trimming, 81-82
nighttime routines, 65-66
obedience sports, 106-107
older dogs, 83-85
parasites, 110-115
patellar luxation, 44, 123
physical characteristics, 6, 8
puppies
  feeding, 56, 64-65
  finding, 38, 40-41
  questions regarding, 42-44
  settling in, 59-60
  viewing litters of, 45-46
Rally O, 107
regurgitation, 73
rescued dogs, 36, 66-67
show dogs
  exhibiting, 109
  history of, 14-15
  potential, 29, 47
skin mites, 116-117
skin problems, 121
social skills, 86, 88-90
sporting dogs, 28
stationary exercises, 99-100
temperament, 8-10, 18
ticks, 115, 117
time commitment, 29-30
toys, 56-57
training
  classes for, 91
  clicker, 100
  come when called, 97-99
  good manners, 31-32
  guidelines for, 92-94
  leash, 95-97
  outdoor, 89-90
vaccinations, 89, 112
veterinarians, 59
weight management, 31, 74-75
worms, 113-114
wrinkle cleaning, 82-83
yard safety, 51-52